I'll never look at an onion the same way again! As Bobby shares the thoughtful approach to optimizing the use of an onion, the application for approaching team members with the same care is obvious. Choose carefully—whether it's onions or people—to maximize the final product.

Dan Miller, *New York Times* bestselling author, *48 Days to the Work You Love*

What a fascinating story! Embracing timeless principles from servant leadership to humility makes it no surprise the impact Bobby has had and will continue to have on organizations.

Everyone wants to be a leader until they get into the real work of becoming a leader. What if there was a step-by-step recipe to becoming that leader? In *Cutting Onions*, Bobby Shaw has meticulously given you that recipe. His insights will make you laugh, cry, and give you reason to dig down into the core of leadership which is self-awareness. This book is for anyone who wants to make an impact and become the leader they know they can be.

Donald Burns, The Restaurant Coach™

Any leader at any stage of their career would benefit from reading *Cutting Onions* and asking themselves the questions that Bobby asks. This book is about leadership at its core—you can't fake this. Bobby talks about, "How you get there is just as, if not more, important as getting there." This defines a true leader. I LOVED it!

resident of Marketing,

rcus Hotels & Resorts

T0163692

Bobby's commitment to be an aggressive learner is what continually remakes himself as a progressive leader in an ever-changing marketplace. In hearing him say, "Success is best shared and most things in life are a team sport" is the simple wisdom that separates him from others.

Jim Sheridan, Founder of Sheridan's Frozen Custard
& Sheridan's Unforked

Bobby Shaw is a generational passionate "People First Leader" who is driven by on-going learning and strategically focused on navigating the radical changes impacting the hospitality industry. *Cutting Onions* premise has tremendous applications to all industries trying to compete and be relevant in an ever-changing marketplace.

Mike Zoob, Founder of Hospitality United Group

I bought into Author Shaw, not just his book. Why? After three decades of being an Executive Leader, this book created a conscious shift in my thinking. The opening story of a rock icon Neil Peart and his quest to change his drumming style after he'd achieved the top of his craft shifted my thinking. I related to Bobby's journey from front line staff to top leadership in the restaurant industry. I wrote notes and captured over 14 key leadership concepts that will be helpful in my career and coaching of other people. One thing is for sure, if you let this book open your mind, it is POSSIBLE to change the "Arc of a Leader" no matter what stage of career.

Tom Dutta, Founder and CEO, KRE-AT,
a people development company

CUTTING ONIONS

CUTTING ONIONS

Leadership Lessons Learned
From the Restaurant Industry

BOBBY SHAW

NEW YORK

LONDON • NASHVILLE • MELBOURNE • VANCOUVER

Cutting Onions

Leadership Lessons Learned From the Restaurant Industry

© 2020 Bobby Shaw

Published in New York, New York, by Morgan James Publishing. Morgan James is a trademark of Morgan James, LLC. www.MorganJamesPublishing.com

ISBN 9781642795783 paperback
ISBN 9781642795790 eBook
Library of Congress Control Number: 2019939451

Cover Design by:
Megan Dillon
megan@creativeninjadesigns.com

Interior Design by:
Christopher Kirk
www.GFSstudio.com

Author Bio Photo by:
Homero Cavazos
https://homerocavazos.com/

Morgan James is a proud partner of Habitat for Humanity Peninsula and Greater Williamsburg. Partners in building since 2006.

Get involved today! Visit
MorganJamesPublishing.com/giving-back

This book is dedicated to my wife Evan.

Thank you for your tireless support for this project and encouraging me to finally put pen to paper and get all of these ideas and real-life examples of leadership down in writing. As I have said many times, this journey doesn't happen without you.

To my kids: Jake, Jordan, Joey, Jamisyn, and Jentry.

Thank you for your love and support throughout this project as you've watched me try and live out these principles in my life at work and at home. I've missed a lot over the years and am striving to be here now to walk alongside you on your journeys into leadership.

Table of Contents

Foreword

I have been in leadership for the majority of my career. I founded my first business at age eighteen and sold it nine short years later to a Fortune 500. The sale of my first business was the catalyst that set me in motion to start, acquire, and sell more than a dozen successful companies.

I'm constantly looking for leaders that make a difference—I mean a real, significant difference in the lives of others. Having had hundreds of employees and dozens of top-level executives work with me and for me for four decades, I have the ability to spot a real jewel. Bobby Shaw is that rare treasure. Bobby has many attributes and experience, but what stands out to me is he is a man of character. You can teach someone to do a task, but you can't teach character, honesty, and integrity to the level Bobby possesses it.

I'm the founder of a high-level mastermind that Bobby is involved with called Iron Sharpens Iron. In order to be a member, you must have these qualities and traits. Week after week Bobby subjects himself to the scrutiny of others to grow both personally and professionally. Bobby shows up prepared and ready *for man in the middle*, a hot seat that rips you to shreds if you are neglecting your responsibilities. Bobby is willing to do the hard work and reps that matter so that he's able to show up in the workplace and at home to meet the rigorous demands he's faced with daily. That is a level-five leader.

It's grueling being a top performer, yet year after year Bobby shows up in that position regularly. In this amazing book, *Cutting Onions,* he uses a creative example of peeling back the layers to see or show you what is beneath the surface. Many have facades or a translucent type covering that shields the real deal, hiding in the shadows praying no one discovers the real you. This exercise of removing layer after layer until you arrive at a solid foundation can be painful, to say the least.

If you want better answers, it's incumbent on you to ask better questions. You can't fix something you don't know is broke, so there are complete chapters showing you how to ask the right questions and when, as well as how to diagnose the root cause of the problem. Bobby takes you on a deep dive in so many areas of his book as it relates to becoming a great leader.

So what about you? How many layers of the onion did you peel back when you started your journey that might expose your inadequacies? When I began my career, I had a poker face and a facade that was impenetrable. I didn't want anyone to know anything about me, and I certainly would have never exposed my challenges. To admit ignorance to any leadership skill was taboo, and it wasn't happening. As I matured as a businessman, I discovered that real strength starts with vulnerability and transparency. We all have superpowers and an Achilles heel, but we keep our "heel" tucked back out of reach and out of sight. If you want to develop as an amazing leader and take your life to the next level, I would strongly recommend you take the time to read *Cutting Onions* and make a determination if you need to peel a fraction more.

Aaron Walker
Founder, View From The Top,
Author, *View From The Top*

Acknowledgments

To Art, Wanda, and Brenda–For taking a chance on a sixteen-year old kid in 1984 and seeing something in him that he did not see in himself.

To Matt and Gretchen–For taking that same kid almost twenty years later and believing he was meant to do more and giving him the opportunity to do so.

To Steve and Monty–For the vision of what it means to change the world through the intimate experience of sharing a meal, building a culture, and encouraging me and so many other leaders to change our world through investing in the people around us.

To the hundreds of people who I've been privileged to lead over the years–this story is my story, but it is your story too. Thank you for trusting me to lead you to places we couldn't get to unless together.

To Jim and Chris Howard, my coaches—You pulled something out of me that I would not have been able to communicate otherwise. You invested yourselves in this project and your tireless efforts show up everywhere in this book. I am so grateful to both of you!

To Morgan James Publishing–Thank you for believing that this story matters and that how you build a strong people culture is the foundation of excellence in everything good that happens in our lives. You made the chance to tell this story possible.

Introduction

A Work in Progress

A s I sit down to write this book highlighting the leadership lessons I have learned in the restaurant industry, I still feel like I am learning new things every single day that make me a better leader. I am by no means done! Truly, I am a work in progress. And I think that's the way it should be. If after many years in our chosen field we've achieved a certain level of proficiency, we should be proud of that, but we shouldn't think of ourselves as great—as having arrived. We should strive to be life-long learners, and we should consider ourselves good, aspiring to be great. You might be surprised to find out that this line of thinking was inspired not by a leadership book, but by a Rock and Roll Hall of Fame drummer.

My favorite drummer is Neil Peart of RUSH. Many years ago, he developed a project called *A Work in Progress* which chronicled his new approach to playing the drums after twenty years for the recording of RUSH's sixteenth album, *Test For Echo*.

The title of his project was meant to show that even after playing the drums for decades, he still had more to learn even as an accomplished drummer. He took lessons for the first time. He completely changed his approach to the drums. He changed how he set up his drums. He changed how he sat at his drum kit, and he changed the ends of the sticks he hit the drums with. He even hired a teacher for the first time in his thirty years of playing the drums!

Neil Peart fully embodied the idea that he still had much to learn. He also wanted to get better and not rest on any of his past success. That resonated with me when I first heard him talk about his journey to "learning how to hit things with sticks" back in 1996. Over the years, it made me realize how much more I had to learn, how much better I wanted to be as a leader, and how much more I wanted to develop the people around me.

I have been blessed to lead at a high level in several organizations, experience success, and make an impact on the lives of the people I've worked with, but I, too, am still a work in progress. I have more to learn and do, and staying hungry and humble is the key to continuing the process of learning and getting better.

Being confident enough to inspire a team of people to greatness and being okay with realizing you don't have it all figured out is the secret combination to becoming a leader worth following. As a leader, greatness should elude you. That's good news because once you think you have achieved greatness, you aren't as hungry. At that point, you simply aren't as effective. Surround yourself with people who will challenge you, inspire you, and make you better. Be the leader who is constantly learning, always getting better, and continually elevating those around them.

Chapter 1

The Art of Cutting Onions

You may be asking why I titled this book *Cutting Onions*. Contrary to what that title suggests, this is not a cookbook. It does, however, have a lot to do with my life in the restaurant industry and how the restaurant industry has changed my life. Cutting an onion was one of those foundational skills that I learned at Chipotle, and like Neil Peart taking drum lessons well into his career, I was well into my career before joining Chipotle and learning how to properly cut an onion.

Fast forward several years and I was standing in my kitchen cutting an onion to prep for dinner when I realized that cutting an onion and leadership are very similar. I know you may be asking yourself…cutting onions and leadership? What do they have to do with each other? Let me back up a minute. As I mentioned earlier, many years ago during my time at Chipotle, I learned that how you cut an onion matters. When you cut an onion properly, you have to take your time; you have to show a lot of patience; you have to do it with finesse. You really have to use skill. It's as much about the technique as getting to the end result, and that's the structure of great leadership as well.

How is your leadership influencing those around you? Leaders have to think about how they're going to lead a team, lead a family, or even just lead themselves. You have to think about how you're going to approach leadership and how you're going to execute that leadership.

As a chef, you would never just cut an onion haphazardly. You would think about what you are making and approach the onion in a manner that would produce the best flavor for the dish that is being prepared. Leadership has to be approached the same way. There is a right technique, a right style, and a right attitude for leading your team in the right direction. You can't use a one-size-fits-all approach. It can even be unique to each *individual* you are leading, rather than unique to the situation. Much like with an onion, you may have to alter your technique depending on the onion you are cutting and the dish you are making.

How you do anything affects the end result. You can have the right onion, but if you approach cutting an onion with the wrong technique, it's going to totally damage the onion to the point that it's not really going to be useful in the recipe that you're trying to make.

Let's say that you are preparing onions for salsa or guacamole. The first thing you do is peel the outer skin off the onion. Then you want to cut the onion in half. At this point, you take the time to really look at the onion and see there is natural ribbing in the onion that you can use as your guide. Making small cuts across these ribs will produce a diced onion with perfectly sized onion pieces for your salsa or guacamole.

If you use the wrong cutting method, you will end up with onions that are too big, which will ruin the final product. The onion will overpower the other ingredients. Yes, you'll still be left with salsa, but it won't be very good salsa.

Leadership is no different. If you're leading a team, you have to know what conclusion you are trying to get to and how to lead your team in the best way to accomplish that goal. As a leader, you have to think about the outcome and how each member of your team performs in order to make the end result the best it can be, but you also have to think about how *you* are going to show up and perform too.

Much like when cutting onions, you have to think about how you approach that team. First, you have to pick the right knife because it would never work to cut onions with, let's say, a dinner knife. Knowing what kind of knife you need for the task is critical, and knowing how to pick that right knife is even more important. If you are slicing bread, you would use a serrated bread knife because it holds onto the bread while you're cutting it. If you were cutting an onion, you would use a chef's knife, which gives you more control over the cuts you are making. Then, you have to think about how you hold the knife. It sounds really simple, right? But the specific way you hold the knife is really important because that determines how you control the blade. If your hand is all the way around the handle, you're able to guide the knife with your index finger, which will allow you to move the knife properly, and give you the best control to get the result you want to achieve.

Using the wrong approach when cutting an onion will cause you to lose control. With the wrong approach, as you cut the onion, chunks are going to go all over the cutting board—some may even end up on the floor. You're going to get randomly sized pieces, which will change the consistency of the dish you're making. The technique is critical when it comes to how you pick the knife, hold the knife, direct the knife, and how that knife actually slices through the onion. Just like there is an art to cutting onions in order to get what you want to have in your recipe, the same goes for leadership. There is an art to it!

While holding the knife correctly is a huge factor in producing the right kind of onion cuts, just as important is the shape of the knife. Your knife has to be in top shape to perform properly. It must be clean and sharp. You want your knife to be able to cut through the onion so crisply and easily that you're able to retain the natural juice in the onion.

You could do everything right from a technique point of view, but if you use a dull knife, guess what? It's not going to turn out the way you wanted it to. You began with a tool that was not going to be able to get you the desired result you wanted, so no matter what you do from that point forward, it's not going to work out the way you had hoped. The same thought process applies in leadership. A leader has to use proper technique with each individual he or she leads. A leader also has to make sure that he or she is using the right tools to get the job done and that those tools are in good shape.

As I stood in my kitchen thinking about how important it was to train a line member to properly cut an onion and how that relates to leadership, the analogy really struck me as incredibly important. While it was extremely important for everyone who worked for me to be able to cut an onion properly, that was just the tip of the iceberg. In order to get a consistent result with the food we were making at Chipotle, the same amount of care had to go into preparing every ingredient we used.

That's true of leadership, as well. Your team has to perform at the highest level in every aspect of their operation for the best result.

How you get there is just as, if not more,
important as getting there.

Most people think the way they dice an onion doesn't really matter, but the way you cut an onion can make or break the meal you're making—just like the way you lead will impact the performance of your entire team.

You can ask someone to get a specific result, and they may get it. But the way in which they get that result is either going to be good, efficient, and beneficial for the team's desired outcome, or it's going to be a struggle, taking too much time for that person to *figure out* what to do.

I like to think of a dynasty versus a flash in the pan. A dynasty is the team that you see get it right all the time, while the flash in the pan team can get it right, but they may or may not be able to repeat their success. That's the difference between a restaurant that gives you the same quality service and meal over and over versus one that provides unpredictable service or inconsistent food quality and taste. As a customer, you're not going to be happy with inconsistency. That's why understanding the art of what you do and doing things the right way each and every time is crucial. You have to have a consistent result.

No one wants to be a one-hit wonder. Your results need to be reproducible and predictable, whether you are thinking about cutting an onion, leading your team, or leading yourself. When you show someone how to cut an onion correctly every time they are in the kitchen, they're going to get the result they (and you) want—consistently.

Pulling Back the Layers

You can't get into an onion discussion and not talk about the importance of layers, which happens to be another strong correlation between cutting onions and leadership. On the surface, onions aren't ready to eat or use in a recipe. You have to peel back the outer layer to get to the good stuff. As leaders, sometimes we have to dig a little deeper into what we're doing and who we're doing it with to get the best result.

When you grab an onion straight out of a bag, it's never ready to use. It's not ready for a recipe; it's not ready to be diced or sliced. The onion is in its most raw form and needs to be prepared for the dish it's going to be used in much like new leaders need to be prepared for their roles. They don't know what you know, and they're not ready to be in the mix. They need to be developed. They need to be taught. They need to be trained. You have to prepare the onion just like you must prepare a leader. It's important to get under those layers and find the good stuff to work with.

When you peel back the dry outer skin of an onion, you'll often find some blemishes on the flesh of the onion, but as you continue to peel off each layer, you'll see the onion gets better as you go deeper. Sometimes you have to dig deep to get to the onion you want. But here's the thing: when removing layers and getting below the surface, it's also important to not take too many layers off. We want the onion to maintain its individuality, and we want a leader to do the same.

Keeping the Core Intact

The thing about an onion is that you cannot see the core until you get inside. You can see where they pulled it out of the ground, but it's only when you pull back the layers and get to the center of the onion that you discover the core.

No two onions have the same size core. Each onion has the right core for that particular onion. Each onion has the root that it needs in order to become the onion that it is. It has the right root system to have supported that onion during its development. Likewise, it's so important to maintain the root and the core in leadership because the root grounds who you are. It makes you who you are as a leader, and it makes that onion what it is as an onion.

You never, ever remove the core. The core holds everything together. If when cutting an onion the core is removed, the onion is going to fall apart.

When you're dicing an onion for salsa or guacamole, you need the core to hold it together. The core has to remain intact so that as you cut through the onion, you're able to maintain the control and get the right size cut for what your recipe needs. Knowing where you came from as a leader and knowing how you got to where you are (your "core") is incredibly important in leadership.

If a person's root is really grounded and the core is holding that individual together, it's going to allow them to be the best version of who they already are. Many times in leadership you'll hear things like, *you can be anything you want to be*, but that's not exactly true. You can certainly be a better version of who you already are, but you really need an understanding of who you are, where you came from, and what it is that drives you. You need to know what your core values are (pun intended) and what it is that actually holds you together as a leader.

How often do we see great teams whose strong, consistent results fall apart when the core is messed with or removed? The effects of that can spread throughout an entire team.

I've seen this happen over the years when there is a core team in a restaurant, and when you mess with that team, you also mess with the restaurant's results. If you take someone out of the team without replacing his with someone just as strong or stronger, the team falls apart.

So when you're cutting an onion, make sure you choose the right onion. You need to know exactly how to cut that onion properly to prepare it for the recipe you're making. You want to peel back the layers to get the best part of the onion, and then you want to make sure you keep the core intact so that the onion stays together while you make the best cuts for your recipe.

As a leader, you want to make sure you choose the right people to be on your team. This doesn't mean that they need to be carbon copies of yourself. You need people who share your core values but also have diverse viewpoints to challenge your thinking and help you be the best version of yourself. You need to lead those around you to discover the best versions of themselves and prepare them to perform at the highest level possible. And you want to create a core system that makes it easy to consistently get the results you desire.

Chapter 2

What is Leadership

Leadership is a huge topic and there are countless books with endless ways of describing it. It seems like every thought leader out there has his or her own unique way of looking at this important topic.

I don't want to make this difficult or complicated. In fact, I want to describe leadership in as clear a way as possible. I look at leadership not through the eyes of an intellect who has studied leadership for years and years and is trying to write the next great thesis about how a new model of leadership is needed, but rather from the eyes of someone who has worked in an industry for years and years drawing the most out of every team I've encountered.

I have worked in the fast-food restaurant industry for most of my life. I've worked at every level from line cook to CEO. From my experience, I have concluded that author Andy Stanley is right: leadership is really made up of three things.

It's Influence.
It's Stewardship.
It's Temporary.

Leadership is Influence

Years ago, I heard a talk by John Maxwell, an incredible author and leader who has had a huge influence on me. When listening to him, I really began to understand leadership in the right terms. Leadership is a big word. It encompasses a lot and can be hard to define in simple words, but I want to take the next few pages and lay out what I believe leadership is at its core.

First and foremost, leadership is influence. As a leader, you have the opportunity to be a positive influence, but you also have the same opportunity to be a negative influence. The good news is that you get to choose. Be a strong leader and do things right, and you will impact the people around you for the better.

There have been quite a few times in my career when someone has invested in me, and that investment has influenced me. The first time that someone in a leadership role influenced me was when I was working at McDonald's as a young crewmember in 1984. I was working in the kitchen, and I was asked to come up to the front counter to take orders, which is not something I ever wanted to do or thought I would be asked to do.

Going up to the front counter may not sound like that big of a deal, but what you don't know—and can't tell—from this book is that I grew up with a pronounced stutter that made it very difficult for me to communicate as easily as I would have liked in those early days. Everyone I worked with knew that, and they were very supportive. I was comfortable working in the kitchen where my communication was limited to a smaller setting with people who knew and accepted my stutter. I had never prepared to work on the register where I had to talk to people who didn't know me, and I never had plans of doing so.

I was working a dinner shift one night when my manager, Brenda, called back to the kitchen and asked if I would come up front. She could see that I was really nervous and not feeling good about this at all. I remember telling her that I wasn't the right person. But she told me it would be fine. She said it was really slow that night and that she'd be up there with me the entire time. She assured me she would be right behind me and that she would back me up. She told me she would help get all the orders, and that if I had any problems, she would also help with the guests.

I remember walking up there, asking myself what in the world I was doing. But true to her word, Brenda was right behind me the entire time. She backed me up. She was there for me when I had questions. She was there for me when I struggled. That was the first time someone invested in me and used her influence to get me to do something that, to be honest, I didn't think I would ever be able to do. My life changed that night because of that simple act of kindness and small investment in me. I rode my bike home, so excited to tell my mom I had worked the register and interacted with customers. I couldn't have dreamed such a simple experience that night in 1984 would change the trajectory of my life.

That was such a great example of real leadership. People often think of leadership as being in a position or having control, but **real, powerful leadership is leveraging your influence to get others to do more than they thought they could**. To be an effective leader, you have to do things in such a way that others around you want to follow you. They want to be better because you're better. That starts with you seeing something in someone that they don't see in themselves.

Leadership is Stewardship

When most people think about stewardship, they think of guarding or protecting something of importance, but stewardship is as much about giving as it is protecting. It's about giving in the right way—giving with the right mindset and giving to the right people. You have to look at leadership in the same way. You want to be a good steward of it or else you will cease to be an effective leader. You can't hold back on leadership. You have to be willing to freely offer it to everyone on your team without wondering if or when you're going to get a return.

When you're being a good steward of your leadership, you're not worried about the rewards. It's not about you. You're worried about the other person, the individual who you're leading.

I believe that to him whom much is given, much is required. I understand that's also true of leadership. You have a responsibility to invest in the people around you, much like Brenda invested in me.

Stewardship is not just about giving your efforts; *how* you give your efforts is just as important. Influence is only one resource that you have available as a leader. You have your influence, skill abilities, time, finances, and energy. All of these are used together to create effective leadership. It's how you use those resources that make the difference between great leadership and not-so-great leadership. You have to be a good steward of those intangible resources that are unique to you and limited in volume. This is apparent in my story about Brenda. She was really using her leadership as stewardship, which is incredibly powerful because when you look at leadership and you think about your resources, you have to be mindful of how to best use them.

For instance, Brenda chose a time that was appropriate. We were slow that night, and she knew that I wouldn't get overwhelmed. She also knew she'd have time to stay close in case I needed her help. Because of that, she was not in danger of overwhelming herself in that situation either.

When you're using any resource, it depletes over time. You've got to use those resources wisely, and she did a great job of that. People who have been in leadership roles for any length of time realize they must be the stewards of those resources.

Oftentimes, people will say they give 110 percent, but when you get to that point as a leader, you're putting yourself in a dangerous situation. You can give too much and not have enough left for yourself. In order to lead others well, you have to lead yourself well.

You never want to find yourself suddenly running out of gas. Everyone has a cup, and if that cup has nothing in it, you have nothing left to give. But if that cup is so full that it overflows, then everyone around you has an opportunity to fill his or her cups from your overflow. You see, it's not my job to fill your cup. It's my job to keep filling my cup so full that hopefully you can benefit from it too.

So what does that look like in real life? Is that getting time away? Is it education? Is it all the above? Yes. This is extremely important, because we always think about leadership development in terms of what we're doing to develop the people around us, but we rarely think about it in terms of what we're doing to develop ourselves or whom we're asking to help develop us.

I think it's imperative that, as a leader, you have a mentor—someone who can pour into you as you pour into others. It's important that you figure out what leadership resources you can consume that will provide you with fresh and new ideas. This will motivate you to continue making a difference. I personally like reading books, listening to podcasts, and attending conferences and seminars to learn more about what it is that I am passionate about. Being a good steward of leadership is about how we invest in our personal development as much as it is about how we invest in our teams.

Leadership is Temporary

I've seen so many people who get into a leadership position for the first time and think they're bulletproof. They've made it to the top, and that's the end of the story when the reality is that all leadership is temporary. Nobody is the leader permanently. That's one of the things that helped me in my journey as a leader; realizing that my leadership is temporary gives me a sense of urgency. It helps me move with a purpose and be more intentional in what I do and how I spend my time.

Because I know that my time as a leader on any team is temporary, I protect my priorities, including my calendar. I now do things more intentionally because I know I have a limited amount of time to influence the people around me. When time is treated with that sense of urgency, what I find is that it provides an opportunity for me to have a greater impact than I would if I just went about my daily life, assuming that I'm always going to be the leader.

There has to be a sense of urgency, and if you're going to be as impactful and as effective of a leader as you can be, that limited amount of time that you spend with people has to be quality time.

Developing Your Next Generation Leader

If you really understand that leadership is stewardship, and if you really understand that leadership is temporary, you have to be thinking about who's next. You have to think about the next generation leader and what you're going to do to develop them. What are you going to invest in them, and how are you going to bring them alongside you to make sure they're learning everything they need to know to lead at a higher level?

One of the things that I address when I give talks on leadership is that **it's your job to develop someone to replace you**. You want that someone to be as good or better than you are. One of the truest ways to evaluate the effectiveness of a leader is by the amount of other high-performing leaders they have developed. I learned this truth during my time at Chipotle, and it was one of the cornerstones of our people development strategy that allowed us to scale the concept so aggressively.

Don't get me wrong: you must have results too. I don't want you to think that accomplishing your goals for your organization is secondary to building new leaders, but the people you are training are going to get those results better if they are being built to be the best they can be. If you're really developing the team around you the right way, you will never have to ask them to be better. Your team will perform at a high level, and there will not be an issue with results. The results are just going to be there. As with most aspects of leadership, *how* you get there is just as important as getting there.

In the context of the restaurant space, I have a rule: no matter how good you look on paper in your current role, you cannot get promoted or take on a new role unless you have someone who could step into your role and be as good or better than you are. Early in my journey, I remember saying no to some talented people taking the next step in their careers because they had not developed their replacement. As hard as that was, it made them better, and it made me better too.

When you have those immense expectations and standards, it raises the bar and people learn very quickly that it's not about them, it's about their teams. It's about the people around them and their ability to develop other leaders.

Don't Fear the Young Rock Star

Too many people will get nervous after reading that last section. For some, the idea of training others to be better than they are is threatening, but I can tell you that it's probably the most important part of building a successful team. Here's why: the person who doesn't want to surround himself with people who are better than him, or who doesn't want anyone to know more than he or she knows is who I like to call the **unenlightened leader**. An unenlightened leader is somebody who is holding on to control too tightly. They may be getting good results short-term, but the reality is that, in the long run, they're going to lose their best people. This creates a scenario where a leader is only training people to be excellent for someone else's team.

Fear can cripple an organization. When you operate from a place of fear rather than confidence, you don't surround yourself with the best possible people. You can't grow and get the results you want that way.

The enlightened leader recognizes that his or her job is to develop the people around them to be the best they can be. This will not only make your job easier as a leader, but it makes it more gratifying. You begin changing the lives of those you are leading, giving them more opportunities for advancement and growth, and, in return, you will get the best effort they have to offer. The best part of this is that you eventually begin to create a culture in which every leader has the same mentality. Now your whole leadership team is looking to build up the next great leader. And when you do that, everyone gets better.

Delegate Responsibility, Not Accountability

One of the best parts about building a team full of people who are as good as you or better than you is being able to rely on them to shoulder some of the load you carry. You no longer have to do it all yourself, and that's a beautiful thing.

Being able to delegate some responsibilities frees you up to do other things. Having trust that others will be able to do certain tasks as well as you could will give you enough confidence to keep you from worrying about the job being done right.

But that delegation comes with a warning: there is a fine line that you never want to cross as a leader. You can delegate responsibilities, but you can't delegate accountability. As the leader, you are the one who is ultimately responsible for the organizational results, and you have to take that seriously. You want to hold your team accountable when they make mistakes, but when it comes time to own up for the team's shortcomings, it's you who takes the blame as the leader. When things go well, you give the credit to your team. That's what great leaders do!

Remember that you are also training new leaders for your team, and they are always watching you. You've brought them alongside you. They're right there with you and you're right there with them, so they're seeing everything you see. They're hearing everything that you hear. They're seeing how you respond to things that they don't go well. They're seeing how you respond to things that do go well. These are important leadership lessons for them.

It's really a beautiful thing because you're bringing that upcoming leader alongside you, and you're able to model true leadership for them. When you're doing this in the right way, something magical happens. The people you are leading will feel so much responsibility that they will want to be accountable. When they start taking on more of the accountability along with the responsibility, that's when you know they're ready. That's when you know they have become true leaders.

Chapter 3

Making Magic

n the last chapter we talked about delegating responsibility, not accountability, and we talked about how truly enlightened leaders bring someone alongside them to mentor. How does that process start? How do you find out if someone is leadership material in the first place and, more importantly, how do you know you can work closely with that person long enough to impact him and his future?

It all starts with a conversation—just a simple conversation. I prefer to have these leadership conversations outside of my office. I want to go somewhere less official, somewhere where the person I'm talking to can relax and be comfortable. You should pick a place that's outside of where you conduct your day-to-day business. There are too many distractions in a daily office setting that can pull your attention away from the conversation. You want to be able to really lean in and focus on the person you're talking to. Be engaged. Silence your phone and put it away—not just upside down on the table!

Take the time to sit across the table from people and ask them about their hopes and dreams. What are they passionate about? What do they want to do? Where do they see themselves in six months? A year? Two years? Three years? The power of that conversation can be incredible. This will likely be the first time someone in a leadership role has ever done that for them. I recently sat down with a team of leaders I am consulting with and had this conversation; it was the first time anyone had ever done that, and it was incredibly powerful.

The Power of Leadership Conversation

Sometimes we overlook the power that kind of conversation can have for someone. When you take time to sit down with a person, leaning in and writing down the things they are saying, you are showing them they are important.

One of the tools we used at Chipotle was a development journal. They were simple journals that gave us a way to document the leadership conversations we had with our team members. We could take notes during a conversation and keep track of the people who wanted to grow their career, have more responsibilities, and move to the next step. This information can be crucial in building the right team because it helps you confirm that you have the right people in the right positions at the right time.

Getting the Most from The Least

One of the biggest advantages any team can have is getting the most from every single team member. While that seems to be common sense—and it is—it's not something that very many companies take the time to do. Make sure to take the development approach across your entire organization. Don't focus on just the people you think are going to have the best conversations with you. Where the real magic happens is when you find the person who may seem to be the least likely to succeed on paper, but through these deep conversations winds up becoming your MVP. It's finding the diamond in the rough.

When you sit down with that person and have that one-on-one conversation, all of the sudden, you begin to peel the layers back and understand who that person really is. You begin to understand what it is they want to do and who they want to become.

You could very well be the first person
to ever invest time in that person.

That's my own story. I was the least likely candidate to put at the front counter, but because Brenda invested her time and confidence in me, she absolutely impacted my ability to grow as a leader.

It doesn't matter if we're talking about teams in a non-profit organization, teams in a company or a restaurant, or teams on an athletic field. At any given time, we can get so enamored by the superstar that it's hard to see the rest of the team. The superstars are the ones who have those natural abilities, and we're just kind of drawn to them like a moth to a flame. But it speaks much higher volumes when you can get the most out of the team member you least expect results from. When you have true high performance from top to bottom, your overall team effectiveness just explodes.

If you really believe that you're only as great as the person on your team who is the newest or weakest, go spend time with that person first. Really understand them. Do you know how their training went? How were they on-boarded? How are they being treated? What are they getting from this entire experience? This can give you a baseline for how conversations with the rest of the team will go.

Whenever I visited restaurants, I'd want to spend time with everyone on the team, but I would almost always want to talk to the newest person first. I did that because I wanted to see how well we were really doing in terms of training and onboarding and also see how they were fitting in with the rest of the team. This would give me great insight into the culture of that restaurant.

When you flip the script and make time for the newest or weakest person first, it's easy to talk to everyone else afterwards. Go have that first conversation and spend time with that person—invest in them and figure out how you can help them. When you do that, you might just help someone see an opportunity they didn't see before.

You might see something in them that they didn't see in themselves. Again, that's exactly my story with Brenda. I worked hard; I came in early; I always worked my shifts. All those things got me to the point where Brenda decided that she wanted to give me a shot on the front counter. She didn't have to do that, but she saw something in me that I didn't see in myself. I was happy to be working in the role I was in, but when she saw more in me and acted on it, it changed my life. New opportunities were created for me that I would have never considered on my own. That is what great leaders do. They create opportunities for top performers that may not have otherwise existed.

Chapter 4

Building the Best Team

There's a phrase that I've heard some successful people use, and I've never believed in it: *self-made success*. We've all heard someone use that expression, but I really don't think such a thing exists. I honestly believe that behind any successful person, somewhere down the line, there was a team, a leader, or a person of influence who helped them along the way. There was someone who supported them, encouraged them, or lent a hand to them to where they are today.

Success is not an individual sport—it's a team sport. It's not only important to have teamwork, but it's also critical to make sure you have a great team, and to have the right team, you have to have the right individuals in the right place on your team.

A lot of times people struggle with this, saying, "Gosh, I wish the team was better in my organization. I wish we could get better results."

But when you start to look at their individual teams, you realize the problem starts with them not having all the right people, or not having the right people doing the right things.

Having a great team is essential, and how you put that team together—how you build that team—is what separates the championship teams from the mediocre teams. So how do you get there? How do you make sure that you have great team members? How do you make sure you have put together a team that's going to get you the end result you're looking for?

It starts with really understanding what people are good at. You want to know what each person's strengths are and how he or she can best contribute to the overall team. When team members work within their strength zones, they're able to come in and contribute every day with ease and enjoyment.

Each team member should love what he or she is doing. When people are happy and doing what they are good at, they will do a better job. Here's the best part: not only will they be doing a great job individually, but their efforts (combined with the rest of a team made of individuals doing a great job) will dramatically increase your overall success rate.

---

*Hiring decisions should not be made
by looking at short-term needs alone.*

The long-term outlook must be considered when hiring a new team member. Making sure you have a team that is able to work within the members' strengths—and that you have a nice complement of those strengths across the organization—is going to help you leverage your team dynamic in a big way and for a long time.

Avoid bringing people in just because you have a need. Filling voids is a short-term outlook. While filling voids is sometimes necessary, make sure the people you hire can fill the void with the potential to be helpful in other areas as well. I've always believed in the axiom of running short with people who truly care than being fully staffed with people who aren't committed to excellence. I look for people who have the technical skills to do great work and also whom I think will be able to make the team better with their attitude, commitment to excellence, and strengths. I want to know how this new person can help me with my immediate needs and impact my team in a bigger, better way later, always looking towards the future.

No More Jack-of-All-Trades

The success of a team is really the culmination of a group of individuals who are all using their singular strengths and efforts *together* to accomplish a specific goal.

There was a phrase coined during the last couple of decades when people focused on trying to be great at everything—commonly referred to as a jack-of-all-trades. Even today there is still an undercurrent of needing to be well rounded. But remember that to be a jack-of-all-trades is to be a master of none. There are eight billion people in the world, and everyone has his or her own individual strengths—no one has to be able to do it all.

Think about gears in a machine. Each of the gears in the machine has a series of teeth, or cogs, and those cogs mesh with the next gear's cog and then mesh with the next one. Each gear can be different. A few may be larger in circumference while others may be smaller. There will be some with more cogs and some with less. Those differences—how each individual gear works within the system and how each meshes with the other gears—are what determine the outcome or performance of the machine itself. Things like

speed, torque, and direction all rely on how those individuals perform. The same is true with any team.

When you bring a team of people together who have unique
strengths and talents and you get them moving in the right direction, allowing them to really use their strengths to do what they're
excellent at, you create a well-rounded team. You don't need
a group of well-rounded individuals; you need a well-rounded
team filled with strategically placed *individuals* who are all rock
stars at what they do best. You need people who are excellent in
their roles and who are using their strengths to help you achieve
your objectives.

It's Not About You

Another piece of building the right team is the understanding that
just as you are looking for individuals who can work well together,
you have to be one of those people, too. Leaders have to be able
to take the spotlight off of themselves from time to time and put
it on those around them. I see a lot of leaders work their way up
diligently. They deserve the position that they're in, but very soon
after they get that leadership role or that managerial role, the conversation becomes *look at me, look what I've been able to do, look
how I've been able to do this or that.*

You want to lead from a place of humility. It starts with being
genuinely humble about how you got to where you are, and not in a
self-deprecating way. You don't want to walk around hanging your
head, embarrassed to get accolades, but you do want to be humble
enough to give credit where credit is due.

People often misunderstand the quality of humility, and there's a
lot of strength to be found in it. People view it as a sign of weakness
until they see it really lived out in front of them in the right way. It

becomes a strength because you show you're human. And there's nothing weak about that. In fact, it's very powerful for people to see you in that light. It's not about you; it's about your leadership.

Shining the Light on Others

Being humble allows you to shine the light on others. When you get credit, you shine that light on the people around you and share that spotlight. You make it about the team because, remember, if you've done your job right, you're spending time with them. You're investing in the next generation of leaders, helping them get to the point where they can take on the extra roles and take that next step in their careers.

When you step out of the spotlight and shine that light on other people, it's powerful for them. You have once again modeled what it looks like to have genuine humility and think about somebody besides yourself.

As they start developing their teams, they are going to do the same thing. I saw this all the time in our restaurants. We would go in to recognize a manager for doing an incredible job and reward them. Because of the culture we had set up, the managers would immediately bring their team around and have a big huddle to celebrate that accomplishment. Whatever it was, they would celebrate that achievement together as a team.

When things go right on your team, you should share the credit. If you have a great month, a great quarter, a great year, or a great comment coming in on your website, give that credit to other people on your team. They're the ones who executed the mission. They're the ones who made it happen. Of course, you probably had something to do with it, but it's far more important for you to give that credit away.

It's empowering and almost guarantees the people around you are going to step up and do a better job because they now understand the importance of their roles and they know that when the team wins, they win.

Chapter 5

Teamwork

When we think about all of the individual spaces in which people can lead, whether that's a business, church, non-profit, or anywhere else, the focus should always be on *how can we get as much done as possible*, and *how can we get the best possible results*?

It all goes back to the quality of the teamwork you have built. I caution you not to just gloss over this, which is very easy to do. When it comes to being in a leadership position, you hear about how important teamwork is, but the emphasis is lacking on it being *essential* for success. When you look at any organization, there are a lot of moving parts, and those parts need to work in unison to be effective.

In the early days of my career, I had some success, but I wasn't always able to replicate that success as much as I wanted. Sometimes things went really well, and sometimes they didn't. Something was missing in the way I was building and leading my teams.

While at Chipotle, we began to talk about a concept called *who does what when?* With this approach, it was almost as if someone had turned on that light bulb right above my head, and I thought, "This is it! This is what we need."

The *who does what when* thought process helps you establish clear roles and responsibilities—my missing piece. It helped clearly define what each person needed to do in their position, what their responsibilities were, and what they were going to need to do to get to the next level. Even more importantly, it defined what they needed to be working on in each moment to help impact the team in a positive way. My team rallied around that. They loved it because it took all ambiguity out of what it was that they were doing, and it gave them a roadmap to being able to develop leaders that were as good or better than they were.

There's nothing more powerful than having clearly defined roles for your team and a clear understanding of what they need to do to move forward.

Having the Right People on the Team is Essential

You can have clearly defined roles and responsibilities, and you can even have that done for your entire organization; however, if you don't have the right people on the team, it doesn't really matter.

Having the right people on the team executing those roles and responsibilities is imperative, and it really starts with your overall talent management process—how you recruit, how you interview, how you hire, and how you train has to be the baseline for your organization.

Jim Collins talks about this in *Good to Great*. He does a masterful job talking about being the bus driver of your business. A great bus driver gets the right people on the bus, the wrong people off the bus, and the right people in the right seats. You've got to have the right people on your team first, which sometimes involves getting the wrong people off the bus. This frees up space and energy to focus on the people who are impacting the team in a positive way. Finally, you have to get the right people in the right places. This helps everybody do the right things at the right time, which is also critical to your organizational success.

Too many times you can have the right people on the team, but they're doing the wrong things. That doesn't allow them to work in their strength zone, which can lead to frustration, and their results aren't going to be as good as anyone wants. Sometimes great people leave an organization because they're simply in the wrong role and don't feel like they are a good fit on the team. It's important to have the right people on the team, and it's even more important to have the right people doing the right things on the team.

Seeing the Path Ahead

In order to establish those roles and responsibilities and make sure you have the right people in the right places, you need a roadmap. The roadmap helps define what you expect out of each role; it helps answer the question *what do we have to have done?* and helps you match the answer with an individual.

Once you build a roadmap that clearly defines your goals and everyone in the organization understands their roles and responsibilities, they can truly see the path ahead of them. They know exactly what they need to do, not only for their own development but also for the development of the other people they're working with. Establishing clear roles and responsibility helps the whole team succeed exponentially.

Give Them Confidence

Giving team members clear instruction will allow them to approach their roles differently and approach each task with clarity and confidence. Because they have a roadmap, they'll have the ability to see a little bit into the future. I'll go as far as calling this creating the future, because if they can see what's coming, they can adjust.

Going back to my analogy of the roadmap, if they need to take a detour, they can. If they see an obstacle in front of them that needs to be overcome by going around it or removing it from the map, they'll be able to do that. Providing that roadmap is what a good leader does. I tell the leaders who work with me that it's their job to remove the obstacles from their team.

But you can't do that if you don't have the roadmap. That's true in terms of the strategic plan for the organization, but it's also true in career paths and development plans for people in general. What you teach in leadership roles can spill into not only other aspects of their work life, but their home life too. The ramifications of this are so widespread that you will likely never fully know the difference you've made in their lives as a whole.

This confidence building happens very early in the process. Initially, when you bring new people to the team, having that map will give them a great deal of confidence. It will allow them to think, "Okay, there is a plan here. I know the vision and mission of the organization, and I know where we're going."

As I mentioned earlier, when I evaluate the culture of a restaurant, I want to start by focusing on that newest person on the team. That has always been a good barometer for me for how well we were doing with onboarding people and how well we were doing helping them understand the mission in the restaurant.

Having a roadmap increases your confidence as a leader, too. As you continue to advance and grow as a leader, having that roadmap gives you a great deal of assurance that you're going to be able to replicate yourself. You're going to be able to develop yourself and your replacement.

That solid roadmap really gives everyone a lot of confidence. As you begin to show the results of the team's efforts, and you begin to achieve the things you need to do, everyone on the team will get more confident and determined because they know they're not just achieving those things that needed to be done, but they also know they're achieving them the *right way*.

If you haven't caught on by now, *how* you get to your destination is just as important as getting there. A roadmap will help you ensure that you get there the right way. Creating this team morale of confidence, from the top-level leadership of the organization to the newest person on the team, will give you a resoluteness most companies only hope for.

Empowering the Right People, the Right Way

Empowerment is a word that is used a lot when talking about leadership. It's become a buzzword, but it is critical to your leadership success. Empowerment just needs to happen in the right way. To empower someone is to make them stronger and more confident; therefore, the confidence you've gained from creating a roadmap for success gives you permission to empower the team you're developing. I've learned over the years that great leaders truly do empower others. You have to empower the people around you, or you may look around one day to find yourself alone as a leader.

But here's where confidence affects your ability to execute at a high level. You only want to empower people who have high standards—people who know what path they're on, are getting the results the right way, and have the right road map. Imagine having a map with you that you think is taking you to your desired destination, but you are going the polar opposite direction. You'll get somewhere, but you'll never get to where you want to go.

If you empower people who don't have those high standards, it can be very dangerous. If you empower people who haven't been trained, who don't understand the objectives, you've given license to someone to go do something that could be detrimental to the team. And ultimately, that wouldn't be their fault; that's your fault as a leader. When you choose to empower those leaders around you, which you absolutely have to do, make sure they have your same standards and they know the exact direction they're going.

While the United States Army's definition of leadership doesn't specifically use the word empowerment, it's all about empowerment: the process of influencing people by providing purpose, direction, and motivation, while operating to accomplish the mission and improve the organization.

As the leader of your team, you have the ability to help each member find the leader within. Never take that responsibility lightly.

Chapter 6

How to Get from There to Here

When you enter an address into a GPS system, the system creates a lined path to show you where to go. That's a roadmap. It's an overview of the trip and shows you which direction you need to go in order to get to your destination. What happens when you press the "Go" or "Start" button? Well, most GPS systems will zoom in and show you a street-level view of the trip. Meaning, it's going to give you step-by-step, exact directions of what to do where and when.

That same *zooming in* action needs to happen with the roadmap you create for your business or organization. You need to provide your team with a more detailed path. Drill down another level or two, and make sure that some of the high-level ideas and concepts you've introduced are broken down into easy-to-follow steps. For instance, if part of your roadmap says, *empower your team,* what exactly does that mean? More importantly, how exactly do you do that?

When I hired someone at a restaurant, it was never enough to just to hand them the roadmap and a give them a really great orientation. I couldn't simply present them with the vision of the organization and our promise to the customer and then turn them loose in the kitchen. That would have been a disaster.

New employees have to know exactly what to do and when to do it. If I had let my new employees go on their own after just an orientation, and I didn't do anything to teach them their station, they would never succeed. For instance, if I was going to teach someone how to grill steak, and I just gave him a lofty, over-the-top vision statement—talking about how great we were—but didn't show him how to cook the steak, do you think we would have gotten a great steak? No way!

Detailed instructions, a walk-through of the process, and hands-on training are imperative. Once you know they've been trained and know the standards and expectations of their roles, you can let them go and encourage them to move forward to work alongside someone who can train them and ensure they are successful.

Don't let undeclared expectations be your downfall. Just because you hire someone who has held the same role somewhere else doesn't mean you can throw him or her out there without the proper training specific to your organization. If you do, it shouldn't surprise you when you don't get exactly what you want from these hires. Sometimes experience is overrated, and people fail when they aren't told what is truly expected of them.

It sounds like a simple thing, but everyone on a team and within an organization has to have clearly defined roles. There must also be a culture of accountability around those roles. People can't execute instructions when they aren't very clear on what they are supposed to be doing. When you give someone something to do, don't do so lightly. Ask them to clarify what you are asking them to do. This takes only a little time in the beginning to ensure you get the desired result rather than hoping they "get it" and continuing to spin your wheels when they don't.

Who's Next?

One of the major advantages of training each member of your team well is that they will know how what they do affects the next person in line. That could affect the overall outcome of the product you're producing or the efficiency in which it is produced.

Every team member should know it is their
responsibility, whether they're the newest person
on the team or they've been around the longest,
to make the people around them better.

The only way you're able to make the people around you better is to actually know what it takes for them to be better. That's why it's so important to give each employee not only the steps to know what they need to do but also how that affects the next step and the one after that. I don't expect someone who is brand new to know every nuance of all roles in the organization, but I certainly want them to feel empowered to learn and understand as much as they can. Typically, there are natural building blocks in place whenever you're teaching someone new, especially in the restaurant industry, but those building blocks are taught from those within the organization who have already walked that path.

If you work in the *back of the house*, meaning you prepare the food, you're typically going to start out working in prep. You will be prepping food for either the rest of the line if you're in a short order restaurant or for the chef if you're working in a fine dining restaurant. You'll start out on prep because that's really the foundational role of understanding how things work in a restaurant. *How big are those onions really supposed to be? How should I be cutting these peppers? What happens if I don't cut them right? What happens to the finished product?*

This is true in any organization. The way one person handles their responsibilities will affect the rest of the process. It's incredibly important that each team member know exactly what they need to do and why, and it's just as important that they know and realize how that affects the steps ahead, even when they aren't directly involved in those steps. The great thing is, when you've done your job right as the leader, you will have clearly defined roles and everyone will know what they need to do.

This opens an opportunity for the team members to support one another in a very strong way. Individuals will start to find ways to do their job better and see ways other members may be able to do a better job as well. This is what top performers do. Leaders can't do it all alone. You need to be able to entrust the members of the team you lead to be proactive in making the team better. The leader has to tell everyone on the team directly, "We want you to say something. If you see something, you have to say something." Encouraging team members to speak up if they see something that's not right, or if they see a way to make the process better, is hugely beneficial to the success of the team and shows just how important open communication actually is.

You have to have the culture to support that open communication, which can't be a culture that says, "I've been here longer than you, and you don't tell me what to do." You must cultivate an environment that embraces the feedback, one that allows people to bring up those issues when they see them. This way, everyone gets better, and everyone moves in the same direction. You only get that when you build trust on a team, so the leader has to make sure that not only is that expected, but it's also highly encouraged.

What's the Point?

The point of a journey is never to arrive—because you're never done. When you realize that as a leader, you're going to continue to strive to make things better. It's a great realization because it gives you the chance to invest in more people. You get the chance to develop more teams; you get the chance to see more people advance their careers and achieve their dreams. There's always an opportunity to get better.

The restaurant industry is littered with business concepts that thought they'd made it just before they failed.

People get to a point when they start to think they made it and take their eyes off the ball. They stop putting emphasis on getting better, and complacency is the enemy of a great idea.

That's why I say the point of the journey is not to arrive; the point of the journey is to continue to get better. When you work that way, that's when an organization becomes great. That's when organizations become very successful. No matter how good of a year you have, no matter how much you achieve, there is always more to do. When you have that mindset, you won't get complacent.

The other side of that is that you do want to celebrate those things you've done well. You certainly want to take a moment to recognize everyone in the organization for what they've done to contribute. That's the beauty of this whole mantra. By taking the time to celebrate milestones and successes, and at the same time continuing to set new goals and directives, your team is going to respond by sharing that with the people they are working with.

When you say, "This was great so let's celebrate, but I know there's more that we could do," your team will have already beat you to the punch because you have built a culture that believes you never arrive. Your team will know there's always one more person to develop, there's always a way to improve the recipe, and there's always a way to make something better. And when you have that mindset, you don't get stagnant, you don't get complacent, and you don't let your guard down. You don't worry about that new restaurant that just moved in down the street. You stay focused on the tasks at hand—making your organization the best it can be— and that is a never-ending process. Your team knows that and will champion the culture!

Who's Next?

Digging in deep with each team member and making sure they know the ins and outs of what they're supposed to do does more than just make the team better. It also makes it easier to find those individuals who go above and beyond their required activities to do more for the organization. Leaders breed leaders, and that's a significant concept for creating long-lasting success.

Throughout my time working with Chipotle, I learned that in order for us to be able to achieve the growth we wanted, we had to develop our talent internally. I mentioned before that one of the things we said was, "No matter how good you are in your role, no matter how great of a manager you are, how great of a general manager you are, whatever it is, you're not really ready to take that next jump, or that next leap in your career, until you develop your replacement."

I remember having conversations with kitchen managers and service managers, saying, "Look, you're really good. Your food is outstanding, but if I promote you, who's taking your place?"

They look at me like, *Well, I'm not sure.*

As we built the career path for our team, we learned very quickly that you've got to develop the people around you to be as good or better than you are. You have to understand that in order for anyone to be great, and be great for a long time, you need to help each other be great. You can't make it about you existing in the current leadership role. Eventually, leaders are going to move on. They're going to be promoted or have to take another role. It's incredibly important for a leader to, number one, identify talent, and then be able to cultivate that talent to allow others to take leadership roles in the future.

The whole concept of being able to develop your replacement is incredibly important, and it really takes the focus off of you as a leader. When it's not about you, you start thinking about who you're going to bring along on the journey with you and who they are going to bring along with them. When your reasoning shifts like that, you start thinking in bigger terms than the current status. You actually start looking far forward to future generations of leadership.

I believe that when a leader gets to this point, they understand how important it is to develop their replacement and their replacement's replacement; there is nothing they can't achieve as they keep that focus on development. It creates a feeling of growth throughout an organization, which in turn, means there are always growth opportunities, helping with things like retention and employee satisfaction.

In 2008, I was promoted to Executive Regional Director at Chipotle, which meant I had to move from Kansas City to Austin. I remember I had to develop my replacement in Kansas City before I went to Austin. The decision was easy because I had groomed my replacement throughout my time there. So when the time came, it all happened organically. It didn't feel forced or strenuous. It was very freeing and giving; it felt generous.

I always wanted to make sure everyone else had a chance to shine, and I think that's what good leaders do. When leaders are thinking about everyone else on the team getting their opportunities, they'll create natural opportunities, and that's a beautiful thing! That inspires the next line of leaders to think and act in similar fashion. People always want to do for others what someone else did for them, and when you provide people with a roadmap and a zoomed-in view of their role in the company, they're able to flourish and support the culture of growth as they constantly seek to do better for the company and themselves.

Chapter 7

Listening to Lead

G ood communication is a must for achieving the fullest amount of success possible. The problem is that when most people hear the term "communication," they think it's about verbally telling someone what they want. But there's another side to communication that, as a leader, you must recognize as just as important.

In order to be a good communicator, you first have to learn how to be an excellent listener. People who listen and, more importantly, people who *really* listen to understand rather than try to find a way to take advantage of the conversation, make the best communicators. Listening is the most important piece of communication, and in today's world full of electronics and distractions, it's a skill that must be mastered by great leaders. People who listen well become more thoughtful and more intentional. They become better leaders.

Listening to Understand

To truly understand, you must pay close attention. And that means you have to be deeply engaged in the conversation. It all comes down to being present. Being present in a conversation means there's nothing else on your mind—you are focused on the person you are speaking with and making them your only priority at that moment. That means your phone is not out, and you won't be distracted by what's going on around you. You're absolutely in that moment, making great eye contact with them and listening to what they are saying. People want to be heard and you are giving that person exactly what they want.

You're truly in the moment, letting them say everything they need to say. That's what arms you with the right words when it's your time to speak. There's no guessing or saying what you think the person might want to hear but making great responses that help the conversation stay healthy and effective.

Being present in a conversation also allows you to be what I call an **active listener**. As an active listener, you realize that people are couching their words. They're not always saying what they *really* want to say. As your active listening skills grow, you'll begin to see the non-verbal cues that give this away, and this will allow you to pull that information out of them. When people shift a lot in their seat, constantly look away, or show signs on their face that maybe they're uncomfortable with the conversation, that generally means there is more to the story than they are saying.

Those non-verbal cues can sometimes communicate more than an entire verbal conversation. There are some really powerful non-verbal cues that, as a leader, you can pick up on if you take the time to look for them. These cues will certainly help you carry the conversation in the right direction.

You can learn a lot from the *way* people say things, too. Recognizing *how* things are said is incredibly important, because a shift in tone of voice or rate of speed in speech can tip you off to anxiousness or excitement that the person you're speaking with may be feeling. Someone could say all the right words, but the way they're saying them could tell me they don't really believe what they're saying. It tells me there's more to the conversation than they've actually said so far.

If you *want* to have great communication with your team, you need to listen more than you speak, and you need to be fully present in those conversations so that you understand enough to make sure the conversation is beneficial for everyone. It sounds simple, but in today's crazy, fast-paced world, this is truly a learned skill that can make all the difference for you in your leadership role.

The Uncomfortable Silence

Sometimes for great communication to occur, you have to get comfortable with being uncomfortable. In order to listen to understand, you have to let people say what they need to say, answer the question you asked them, or pick up on those cues discussed above. And to do that, you have to be quiet. Really quiet. Uncomfortably quiet!

For a lot of leaders, that's not an easy thing to do, but you have to get used to it. Leaders are used to being the one doing all the talking, being the communicator, the one trying to cast a vision or inspiring the person you're talking to.

Sometimes what you need to do is simply keep your mouth shut and allow the uncomfortable silence.

Don't try to fill the gap. Don't try to fill the silence with unnecessary words. Don't try to fill in what you think the person you're talking to is going to say. When you do that, you're changing the conversation, and it raises the question of, *are you trying to convince them or yourself of what it is your communicating?* More accurately, you're derailing that conversation, because you're not allowing them to communicate what they want.

The silence you grant in the conversation lets the person who's speaking think about what it was they just said. I've been in a number of conversations where the words came out of someone's mouth and ten seconds later they said, "Well, actually, here's what I really mean."

And then they say it more clearly.

That uncomfortable silence that we hate so much is necessary, because it gives the person you're talking to time to think about what they just said; it also allows you as the listener to absorb the content of the communication more accurately. One thing I recommend is taking notes when you're sitting down with someone. This can offset the need to jump in and speak out of turn. It also shows how much you care and gives you the ability to document parts of the conversation, so you have a record of what was said.

One of the negative effects of being a gap-filler is that it can appear as if you're trying to control the direction of the conversation, or it can seem like you're even trying to sway the conversation into a different direction. People might perceive that you're trying to control the story, instead of letting them tell their story. That can have a big, negative effect on the outcome of the conversation.

Another adverse effect is that you can shut down the other person, making them think you don't really value their input. If they think you already know everything about what it is they're trying to say, they immediately start to wonder, "What value do I have to add to this? What can I possibly share that this person doesn't already know, or what can I conceivably share that's going make a difference if they already think they know the answer?"

I've seen this from many high-level leaders over the years, and it's really frustrating to watch because they are undermining the idea that what someone else says is important. You can't say one thing (what you say is important) but let your behavior as a leader say something completely different (what you say is not important enough for me to patiently listen). If you tell people you want to hear what they have to say, you must give them the space and the time to do just that.

Being a gap-filler robs people trying to tell you their stories. You cheat them of a really important developmental opportunity: learning how to engage their boss. You teach them that leadership doesn't really care about them as much as they say they do. Instead, you should listen to them and let the uncomfortable silence do its job. You have a chance to cultivate incredible communication skills in each member of your team if you lead by example, but you won't be able to do that as a gap-filler.

The Art of the Question

With enough time and experience, every leader will know when it's the right time to step in and when it's time to remain quiet. You'll know when it's the right time to open your mouth and say something. And when the time is right, **one of the most powerful things you can learn is the art of asking a question**. This really is an art—and a little bit of science, as well.

What you don't want to do is ask that question right off the bat. When the person is done speaking, you don't want to jump right in with a question. This is not an interrogation. It's a conversation.

Take a minute and paraphrase what you just heard them say to you. This is not just for the obvious reason of confirming you understood what you heard, but also because it is a sign of respect for the person who just told you the story.

It's like you're giving some credence to them for being part of the conversation. Even if you don't agree with what they said, you want to validate that they were heard. You're validating that they really were understood, and that's incredibly important. Repeat back, in your own words, what you just heard and see if it resonates with them. You will know if it resonated by the way they respond. If they just sit there without saying or doing anything, what you paraphrased is probably not what they meant. Either they misspoke or you misunderstood, but your paraphrasing will give them a chance to restate their story and make their point more clearly. If you see a nodding head or a smile and you can just feel that positive energy, then you know you're on the right track.

Once you know the conversation is on the correct path, then you want to ask the question. Now, you've probably got some pre-thought-out questions that you need to ask, or you may want to ask for more detail about something that was just discussed, so take the time to do that, but never ask yes or no questions. Yes or no questions limit the response from the other person to two possibilities and blocks them from being able to express his or her thoughts in full.

Ask open-ended questions with a reflection, such as, "You said this about this particular situation, and you said it made you feel this way. Tell me more about that."

When you dig for more information, you'll get more information. They'll be more than happy to tell you what you want to know because they told you the entire story—and you listened.

When you say *tell me more*, typically, the floodgates will open. You're giving them the freedom to express themselves more deeply. They may have initially just given a cursory overview because they don't believe you actually want to know. In some cases, they may not be telling you everything because they think you are pressed for time. But when you say *tell me more about that*, it's really powerful and gives them the chance to go even deeper.

Sometimes you want to ask a question that you already know the answer to. This is something I learned from a great mentor of mine. He could do it in a way that didn't make him look silly and didn't make the person on the other end of the conversation look foolish. The key to asking a question you already know the answer to is remembering that you're not asking that question for your benefit; you're asking the question for their benefit. You get a chance to hear what they have to say and learn how deep their knowledge really goes on a particular topic. You get to see if they really understand the why behind what the team is trying to accomplish.

And then lastly, you may want to ask a question for the sole purpose of planting a seed. This is where leadership gets kicked up a notch. You're not giving them the answers but rather challenging them to work towards an answer on their own. These kinds of questions will get them to think about the potential ways they're going to solve whatever problem it is that they might have. More importantly, it helps them own that solution, and that's what you want as a leader.

You don't want to be the boss who has to tell everyone how to fix their problems. Instead, help build that skillset in the people you're working with, help them learn how to solve their own problems because then they're going to own those solutions.

Leaders sometimes get bogged down because they're trying to solve the problems of the world instead of teaching the people who are working for them to solve problems themselves. Sometimes that spark of learning happens because you simply ask the question and plant a seed for them.

I can't tell you how many times I've been in restaurants and used this tactic to get my team to where they needed to be. Maybe we're discussing a staffing issue, so I ask them some questions about where they were short-staffed and why, what they have tried up to this point, and what type of resources they've used. This was just me planting seeds. Then a few days later, I get a call saying, "Hey, I got this idea about how I want to fix my staffing problem." Boom, boom, boom, they rattle it off, and it's exactly what they need to do.

Talk about empowerment. When you confirm that you agree with someone's solution to the problem, they have the confidence to try to solve the next problem that comes up. This keeps you free to do more of what you are good at rather than keeping you mired down fixing problems that others could easily solve if they were empowered to do so.

Chapter 8

Writing to Lead

We've talked about the importance of listening to lead, but how do you remember what you heard when talking (and listening) to many different team members? How do you keep it all straight? More importantly, how can you translate and communicate what you heard so that it makes sense to others?

If I had to pick just one communication skill you need to master, listening would be it. However, right behind listening is the skill of writing. While speaking is important—you have to be able to communicate verbally—I think there are some really important things about writing that a lot of leaders overlook.

Not everyone is a great writer, but, in this case, you're not necessarily going to be writing for someone else to read. Write for yourself. I've found over the years that when I write for myself, it helps me in a number of ways, such as helping me clear the decks, create inspiration, and become a better leader.

Clearing the Decks

We've all got so much going on in our minds. As a leader, you have a lot on your plate and a lot of things you're responsible for, including people. Taking that time to clear the decks helps you compartmentalize, re-organize, and remember what has occurred that day. It creates an opportunity to clear your mind and allows you to focus on upcoming tasks and new information as they occur.

I keep a couple of different journals—a personal journal and a gratitude journal. I write in each of them almost every day because that allows me to get the happenings of the day out of my head and onto the paper. I know no one else is going to read it. It's just for me. I keep it personal and clear. That way, I can refer back to what I wrote at any time and know exactly what I meant as I wrote it.

Clearing the decks gives you a chance to free up space in your memory, providing room to store more the next day. It can be easy to overload the brain with information and when that happens, you'll get bogged down. No one functions well bogged down. Trust me—it's better to get it in black (or blue) and white and free your brain up to handle whatever comes next. And, as a bonus, what you wrote will always be there for you to refer back to in the future when the need arises.

In the context of leading, there really is power in writing things down. You want to be deliberate about what you put in your journal(s). You want to take the time to make sure all of your thoughts are clear and understandable.

Most times, I write like I talk, which means the words don't always translate as clearly as I'd like. I may write something, read it back, and ask myself, "Okay, is that true? Am I making something worse than it is," or "am I making something better than it is?" Then I reread it, and I might change some things and write it again—just to make sure it's as accurate as possible. My rule of thumb has always been that when I write something down, I want somebody I've never met to be able to read and understand it; someone who is one thousand miles away and may not know any of the people in the story can still understand exactly what I'm saying.

Clarify the Win

Writing can also help you clarify a win. You have goals you want to achieve, and sometimes those goals can get really involved. There may be four or five things on your operational plan for the year that you want to accomplish, but you may need to break those into chunks to make them easier to complete. So clarifying the wins helps you take those key initiatives and break them down into manageable bites for your team.

You're not going to be able to attack everything you need to do for the year all at once, so you've got to clarify exactly what the steps are that will get you from where you are to where you want to be, along with the when, how, and who for each step.

Sometimes you can get lost in your own mission statements. As a leader, you may need to take time to frame, or, in some cases, reframe the mission. You may need to make it a little bit more personalized. Taking the time to write or rewrite your mission statement will help you clarify the win so that everyone on the team knows exactly what the goal is.

For instance at Chipotle, the mission was "to change the way the world thinks about and eats fast food." It's not a long mission statement, but what does it really mean?

We sat down with that mission statement and broke it into more tangible bites:

- *Source the very best ingredients.*
- *Build good relationships with our suppliers and farmers.*
- *Hire the very best people.*
- *Only use the best equipment to prepare the food.*
- *Build restaurants where guests can engage transparently with the team making their food.*

When you start to unpack all the things within and around a mission, that mission becomes much more powerful and achievable.

Creating Inspiration

When I talk about using writing to create inspiration, I'm talking about inspiring myself as much as inspiring other people! If I'm not inspired by what I write, there's no way I'm going to inspire other people. You should inspire yourself as much as you inspire others. The written word is so powerful, and it can be a very effective way to get people to understand what you're trying to communicate and get your team as excited as you are.

Think about how powerful music is. I love focusing on the lyrics. Sometimes they get lost in the music, making them hard to understand, but when you really break down lyrics and look at them apart from the music, you start to view them a different way. That's true with our writing as leaders. You're writing to cast vision, inspire, motivate, and edify people. All too often, those words get lost in the details of daily tasks, so you have to write or rewrite as necessary to make sure your meaning is crystal clear.

Writing details down will also help create your legacy, which can inspire future generations. I remember years ago, when I first became the general manager at McDonald's, I was sitting in my restaurant across the table from my boss's boss. He was such a great guy—Mark Searle was his name. And I remember Mark telling me about business writing.

He said something to me that sticks with me to this day.

He said, "If it's not written down, it didn't really happen."

I thought, "Wow!" While I didn't really know what that meant at twenty-four-years-old, I'm more than twice that age now, and I get it.

As a leader, why wouldn't I want to document everything? Why wouldn't I want to inspire? Why wouldn't I want to create a legacy through written words that help inspire other people who come after me?

That's one of the key reasons I'm writing this book. I want to have the chance to inspire you through telling my story. I get to share my journey—both the stuff I've struggled with and what went well because of the people I surrounded myself with. I get to share that story with you so you can learn and make your journey better. That's what inspires me.

Writing Makes You a Better Leader

When I think about writing, I think about the power behind the written word. As a leader, **the moment you believe what you're saying is true, it becomes very powerful.**

What I mean is that sometimes leaders will say something—they'll make a statement, they'll write it in an email, or they'll put out a newsletter—and what they say is filled with company language. While it could be good stuff, there is no impact. You wonder, *is anyone really listening to what I'm saying? Does anyone really care?*

As the leader, you certainly know all the right things to say. You know the boilerplate language that is used to describe your company. You know the mission and vision, and you can recite them on demand. But do you truly believe that what you know in your head is actually true in your heart? The moment that belief kicks in is the most powerful moment of a leader's life in any company. Many times, that moment you believe what you're saying is true happens when you read back what you just wrote.

When you're transparently writing about where you're at as an organization, the goals you're working on, and trying to break down those larger goals into smaller, manageable bites, that's the moment you can actually see the future. You can see what your organization is going to be able to accomplish. It's the moment when you can't turn back, because your desire to lead your team to greatness is stronger than the pain of getting there.

That moment when, regardless of the circumstances and challenges you may be facing, you know as a leader that what you believe is true, nothing can change that. Embrace the moment. It's in that moment that leadership becomes art—and can change the world.

Writing helps you become a better leader, because it helps you not only frame everything in your business for everyone else, but it also helps you frame everything for yourself. It inspires you when you know that you will inspire others with your writing. There's a sense of responsibility that makes you pour more clarity into what you're saying. And when you're able to tap into that additional need for clarity, it makes you a better leader.

Throughout history, when people wrote, it's been about the past and what we've accomplished and where we've been, but I think it's as much about creating the future as it is about the past. In many ways, you're able to see the future as you create the future, and there's such power in being able to write that down and share that with other people.

You may be saying, "I'm not a writer, and I don't even know what to write."

Whether you want to write a book, a blog post, or just something in your personal journal, write down the story of what happens along your journey through this life. Write what inspires you. The world needs your story. You need your story.

You don't have to write a book. There are a lot of people who have a lot of passion and knowledge and feel they must do something with it, but you can put all of that in a journal or create your own blog. Even if nobody else reads it, it'll help you become a better leader.

Chapter 9

Digging Deep

How you show up to a conversation is an important part of any conversation. How you show up determines whether or not you are starting a conversation that allows you to dig deep and communicate with your team members in a powerful way. It's something that a great leader has to be able to do well. How do you ask a question that is going to be able to get you the answers you need? There is a true art to it.

Many times, you're asking a question that you already know the answer to in order to plant a seed in the mind of the person whom you're developing. That allows you to dig deep and communicate with them. A lot of times people communicate with the intention of what they want to say and how they want to inform the other person, but...

As a leader, what you need to work at is intently trying to understand what it is that they want to tell you.

Start with a question you already know the answer to. You want to try to plant a seed in the mind of the person you're developing to help them solve the issue at hand. One big purpose for asking the right questions is to help the other person own the solution to whatever problem they're trying to resolve or navigate. That only happens when they come up with the resolution themselves. You have to be able to know how to ask those great opener questions that require a longer response than yes or no.

Empower Them

This is your opportunity to let them shine—to let them come up with their own solution. Don't dictate this conversation. Instead, flip the script. Ask a question that you know the answer to in order to get them talking, thinking, and moving in the direction that you want that conversation to flow. This empowers them to create, which gives them the freedom to find those solutions on their own—all through the questions that you're asking.

If we try to resolve the issue they have and don't involve them in the process of solving that problem, that doesn't give them a chance to work through the steps, which can be a dangerous place to be. It creates a culture where people don't know what to do without you telling them. They don't know how to solve problems because you've solved them all for them. The next time an issue like this arises, they'll be in the same position they are now. They'll have to wait for an answer before they can move forward.

When you take the approach of asking those questions that draw solutions out of them, which they can own, you empower them. You're empowering them to go out and solve the problem themselves, and you're helping them understand that they already have the tools, systems, and processes to resolve issues. They just needed a little bit of help getting there.

This is one great way leaders develop other leaders. When you're asking those questions and allowing your team to communicate and follow through in that conversation the way that I'm talking about here, you're actually taking that next step into living leadership out in front of them while bringing them through their growth process, as well.

Communication Mediums

Today, there are many technology options for communicating through any number of different mediums, whether it be email, direct chat messages, Skype, Zoom, phone, in person, etc.

Email is really comfortable for a lot of people because it can be done quickly. You can respond and mark it off your to-do list, but what you don't get with an email is that personal interaction. I can't tell you how many times I've received an email, read it, and without even realizing it, inserted an inflection or tone I assumed was there. You can change the entire attitude of an email just by reading it in the wrong tone or inserting your own meaning behind what someone wrote. And, what you read may not even have been the intention of that person. Then you waste time getting upset over something that is really a non-issue, something that could have been resolved by just picking up the phone.

There's no doubt that it is easier to send a quick email, but there are many times email is used to avoid a confrontation. I can hide behind an email and say what I need to say. I'm not there to see the effect of it on the other end. As a leader, that's a completely counterintuitive way of thinking. You really need to be out in the open for those communication points.

I learned a trick on this subject from an old boss, and it's always worked for me. If there's ever a moment in time where I think, *should I call him*, the answer is yes. It means picking up the phone. It's easy to say, *I'll just shoot him a quick email*, but if the thought crosses your mind that you should call him, it's an easy litmus test that a call is in order.

When on the phone, you can hear others' inflections and tones of voice. You can also pick up on the silences. You can listen to what someone is telling you and the emotion that is behind what they're saying. You can't do that through email. You can read something in an email and interpret it as completely different than the way the other person intended for you to read it, and that gets dangerous.

As we develop leaders, this needs to be a skill they learn, because it's not intuitive to people and not everyone is comfortable with picking up the phone these days. All leaders have to be able to communicate, and they have to be comfortable picking up the phone or sitting down with someone face-to-face to have a real conversation.

When you're talking about something that's important or personal to an individual, face-to-face is always best, even if you must utilize technology to do so. While you certainly want to try to have those conversations in person whenever you can, I know in today's fast-paced business culture, that won't always work. There are so many great mediums out there for face-to-face communications, such as Skype and Zoom. When you are able to see the other person, you can read their body language and see their eyes, which are both important. It's the one-on-one interaction that goes beyond typing so that you get some sort of direct response mechanism in place, whether that's vocal or visual.

Technology as an Accelerator

Technology is great, and while it should never be a replacement for human interaction, it can be an accelerator to help you communicate quickly. You may not be in the same city or state as someone, but through the technology that is available today, you have a way to interact with them in a much more personal way than email. I think about technology in terms of hospitality because a face-to-face conversation is truly a form of hospitality. In whatever business or industry you're in, you should be using technology to accelerate your efforts, but never to replace the personal interaction.

When you sit across the table from a person making eye contact a connection is created that you can't make any other way.

I talked a little bit earlier about how, over the years, it's been my experience that when I meet with leaders in person, it's a more personal way of making a connection that just can't be made any other way, which is really impactful.

Whether it's the CEO or another important figure within a company who takes the time to sit and talk with team members, it elevates the team members' confidence. They know this person really cares what they think because he or she took the time to be there and listen to them. It's on those visits and in those meetings where there is real personal interaction and an opportunity for those team members to share what their team is doing, which is so important in their development as a leader.

You can't get that same effect with technology. That one-on-one, when someone comes into your business and spends time with each person—sitting with a team to understand what's going on—

is irreplaceable. This is the time when you have a great opportunity to be able to dig deeper because you are there in person.

Listen to the *What's Being Said and What Isn't*

When the conversation gets started, it's so hard not to want to think about how you want the people with whom you're speaking to respond. Even with the best of intentions, it's difficult to not chime in, but you have to really listen and understand what it is they're trying to say instead of trying to formulate your response. Sometimes, even though you might be hearing them, you're not really listening to them to understand what it is they're trying to say. Instead, when you're formulating that response in your head, you miss crucial things that are being said.

It's important to clear everything that's on your mind in that moment. I've made mention of hearing the silences in conversations. It can be uncomfortable, but this is where you practice that. This is where you're simply listening and not being a gap-filler. As you do that, you'll begin to notice the cues you get from the person you're speaking with—you see their body language, how they're making eye contact with you or not, and their tone of voice and inflection when they get passionate about something. I think this tells the story just as much as the words themselves. While words are important, these things that help support the conversation are just as significant.

It's necessary to listen for understanding. It's easy to listen in order to find the solution or to find an argument. And, if I'm being honest, this is not just done at work, but even in our own families. If we can turn that part of our mind off and allow ourselves to listen to what's being said for understanding, then we start seeing the real issues that lie underneath what's actually being said.

When we're so sure that we know the answer, we miss the fact that while we might be right, the other person might be right, too. When you enter a conversation thinking you're right, and you're so sure, in fact, that you don't even believe you need to have this conversation, you miss something as a leader. You miss the opportunity to learn something that you might not have learned any other way other than through this conversation. And, that's a big miss.

This can cause a lot of issues because now the conversation could turn emotional and even argumentative. There are a number of negative ways that a conversation can go simply because someone interjects what they assumed was being said as opposed to what was actually being said, and that creates more stumbling blocks than there were before the conversation started.

Earlier, I talked about the importance of being able to remove obstacles. Remove yourself from the equation by truly listening for understanding. You have to be able to do that to hear the whole story.

Everybody has a need and a desire to be understood on all levels—whether it is personally, professionally, within their families, or how they interact as a human being. We look at a structure of an organization and see a lot of names, roles, and positions, but what we don't see is each individual story, and there's a narrative that runs in the life of every single person.

In every conversation you have as a leader, there is a story being told, and it's incumbent upon us as leaders to understand that narrative and be able to dig deeper. We need to be able to fulfill that desire to be understood. We can do that by not only listening but by engaging in that story. There's nothing more powerful. When that CEO or high-level leader comes into the business, and they spend time with the people, the employees feel important and heard because that leader is coming in and connecting with them.

When that happens, you start to understand someone's story; you remember the names of their children and their hobbies. You can ask them about the last conversation you had with them, and you can ask them how their development is going. That's the payoff of listening. When you understand those cues and are able to use that information to help you in future conversations, it's no longer a simple conversation. There's a real narrative in each one that we have to understand as leaders.

When you do this, you take someone from feeling like an employee, or feeling like a number, to feeling like part of the family. And when you get that buy-in, they take ownership of the message. They buy-in deeper to the company's goals, the vision at hand, and they're willing to invest more of their time, effort, and lives into the goal of the organization—simply because they feel so much more integral to its success.

They may believe in the mission, and they may believe in the vision, but they believe in the leader more, and that connection they have with you is so genuine. It's what fuels their desire to go out and try harder to accomplish the mission. Don't underestimate the importance of their connection with you. Research backs up the fact that **people don't leave a company, they leave a boss**. It's almost never the company that they're walking away from. It's always the interaction with that one individual or that team of individuals, when an employee has engaging connection with the leader, and that leader has it with his or her team, that's really hard to break.

When you look at the best-performing organizations out there, the ones that are able to achieve long-term, sustainable success, they are the ones in which employees have that deep connection with the leader, and the leader is engaged in the narrative of his or her team.

Chapter 10

Developing Yourself as a Leader

U p to this point, I have been talking about leadership development in terms of how it pertains to what we are doing for the people around us. That's really important, and I will be coming back to that aspect of leadership, but the other side of the conversation that isn't always talked about is how to develop yourself as a leader. There is arguably more responsibility to develop yourself as a leader than there is for anyone else to develop you, but that doesn't mean you operate in a silo, and it doesn't mean you're on your own.

Sometimes, as a leader, you can feel boxed in, like you're in a glass house. But in reality, you're not a lone ranger. Part of developing yourself as a leader is surrounding yourself with others, people who aren't your boss but who may be trusted advisors, people who can be honest with you and give you the feedback you need to do better. It has to be those who are not afraid to give you honest feedback.

Don't Believe Your Own Hype

You need to have someone in your life—or even a group of folks—who can act as a personal board of directors. It must be people who will speak truth and be honest with you. Outsiders see the blind spots that you can't when you're in the battle. You're the one on the front lines every day, and it's hard to see the forest through the trees.

Leaders get in trouble when they start believing their own hype and think they have it all figured out. It's for that reason you need a trusted advisor to join you on the journey. You need someone who's gone farther than you've gone. There will never come a time that you won't need a mentor. Having one can help you stay sane when things are hard. Every leader needs a good sanity check every once in a while. Involving mentors in your life allows you to vent and have somewhere safe to get frustration out, and they can offer guidance for how to handle a specific situation. When you have people around you who can bring you out of that silo and into the light, it's incredibly helpful.

When thinking about a mentor, people often try to decide who they would want to mentor them, but I think it should be done differently. Instead, find someone who wants to mentor you. When you find that person, someone who sees something in you that maybe you don't see in yourself and invite him into your circle of influence, that's a powerful place and it's where the magic can happen.

Finding someone who wants to mentor you sounds daunting, but it is easier than it sounds. The single biggest thing you can do is to authentically be who you are! Don't try and be someone else. By doing this, you will naturally attract a leader who wants to get to know you better, who sees something in you that might mirror themselves early on in their journey. They will seek you out to help cultivate those things for which they see potential.

If you go into meetings with your mentor and always leave feeling good about yourself, that person is probably the wrong mentor for you. A good mentor might hurt your feelings, but it's because he or she sees things you don't see. If you leave a meeting having received the opposite advice you thought you were going to get, that's usually a good thing. A mentor can help you to clear a path; it just might not be the path that you were hoping or thinking it was going to be.

I'm involved in a high-level mastermind group, and one of my favorite things about this group is not our Monday afternoon meeting, but what happens in-between those meetings. After one of our meetings, one of the guys, whom I trust and respect, got in touch with me and called me out on some things that came up during the meeting. Was I happy to hear those things? Not at first, but in the long run, I knew what he said was right. I needed to slow down a bit, accept the feedback, and take a breather on my idea.

Create Blank Space

It can be very easy to say *I don't have time for that* when it comes to finding a mentor or a mastermind group. When it comes to our schedules, the things that tend to get dropped first are the things that are important to our self-development. You have a busy life with meetings, conference calls, emails, phone calls, and trips—and that's just work stuff. Add things like soccer games, dinner with the family, oh, and let's not forget church and weekends. Our schedules are packed way too full!

I used to be terrible when it came to my calendar as a leader. I felt like if it wasn't completely jam-packed, if I didn't have every hour of every day accounted for, I wasn't doing enough. It made me feel like I wasn't contributing enough—almost like I wasn't doing my job properly. So I packed my schedule way too full.

Don't do that. That's how you end up with a calendar with no time to work on yourself.

Scheduling time for you is not intuitive for most people. It's not something you see as a key business priority, but the reality is that it's the key to being successful as a leader.

I can look back at several points in my life when my schedule just got so full that it didn't allow for time to work on myself, and it wasn't good. You have to be really intentional about scheduling downtime. Juliet Funt, the daughter of Allen Funt from the old television show *Candid Camera,* operates a company based on intentionally scheduling time where you literally don't have anything going on. She's coined it *white space.* It's total downtime. It is time for you to think, write, process an idea, simply read, or whatever you might need—because you do need that time.

Sometimes it's just a little bit to allow yourself to breathe and take a walk. You hear these inspiring stories of leaders who have been working on a project, and they just can't figure it out. They've worked on it for hours, weeks, or even months and months, and then they go take a half-hour walk and, voila, they solve it. Having that intentional downtime allows you to approach the things you're working on with a new perspective and a clear mind.

You have to stop feeling guilty for having downtime on the calendar. You have to get past that feeling and understand that downtime will be what keeps you sane. In reality, it will allow you to be able to achieve more than you ever thought possible. Here's the interesting thing: most leaders would tell you that nobody's telling them they can't schedule that time. It's self-imposed guilt—there's somewhere you need to be, someone who needs you, something you have to be working on. By not taking the time to invest in yourself, you're not able to help people as much as you could if you were to take that time regularly. Recharging your batteries allows for better focus and can elevate you to a whole new level.

Hardly anyone would set out on a road trip without getting the oil changed in your car, checking the tires, making sure there is enough gas in the tank, and ensuring that everything is in that car to get you where you want to go. Yet, with daily life, you just think you can run on empty all the time. Take time to make sure you are geared up both mentally and physically and ready to take on the challenges ahead of you, or else, you're not performing at your best. There is this mentality that you have to always be on the go to achieve your goal, but if you don't take time to recharge yourself, you're not going to perform at a high enough level to ever achieve the goal. You'll just continue scrambling towards it, puttering on empty.

This isn't just about scheduling. You have to make this blank space sacred—nothing gets put into that slot on your calendar. There is no value in putting it on the calendar if you and your staff know you'll cancel it if something comes up. You need to have a conversation with your leadership team about how you collectively handle this in your calendars.

Everybody needs this time and team members need to protect each other's blank spaces. Get it ingrained in the culture of your organization. Then, it just becomes a thing that you do and that's what you teach new team members when they come on board. It's an opportunity for the next-generation leader to understand what this looks like, because people don't innately think about this time as being important. You have to be really intentional about making it part of your leadership culture.

Invest in Yourself

There are a lot of variables when it comes to time because everyone's schedules are different, but as a general rule of thumb, somewhere between eight to ten percent of your time should be intentional downtime, which translates to three to four hours per week for a forty-hour week. Some people like to take it in a block. Maybe it's an afternoon out of the office or coming in late one morning. Take that morning for yourself; it's okay. And, do it on a weekly basis.

I've gotten to the point where I get away from the office for two days on a quarterly basis and just plan. It could be reading or writing, but whatever it is, I use very little technology. It allows me to review the quarter we're in and take a look at the quarter ahead. How are you are doing on your goals and objectives? There is so much that you can get from that. It's a way to invest in you. When you come back, you're inspired, recharged, and ready to go and lead your team. This isn't just for you; it's for them. Your team needs you to do that.

We're often so caught up in what we need to do for our teams that we don't realize one of the things we can do for them is to **get out of their way and let them do their jobs**. And, one of the ways that we do that is making sure we take the appropriate amount of time away from the business.

When it comes to blocking off this time, think about what fulfills you. Is there some way you want to engage in the community that you haven't had the time for? Think of one thing you can do to invest in yourself. Is it serving a local charity? What are you passionate about? It could be taking a class or getting involved in a church project. Maybe it's volunteering for the local food bank. Maybe you want to attend a conference that will inspire your personal leadership journey.

As I write this, I am getting ready to go to a Leadercast conference in Atlanta. I attend this event every year with my best friend from high school. It's a one-day leadership event, but I'm there every single year. That time is on my calendar as blocked space. That conference inspires me in my leadership journey. This time away is going to look different for everyone, but you need to figure out what those things are that you can't stop thinking about—that you really want to learn more about—and that's what you invest your white space in.

I mentioned taking someone with me to the leadership event, and in the context of leadership, this is important. As you begin to invest in your own personal development, take someone along with you who you can begin investing with. That's been a great way to continue the cycle of leadership development, because then, it's not just about you. Not to mention the fact that when you bring someone with you, you're also giving yourself a little bit of accountability. You see a whole circle of personal development here.

If it can be used as a teaching moment, do it! The more you can expose folks to leadership principles and ideas, the more it helps light that fire of leadership in somebody else who wants to learn more. That happens because you chose to involve and engage them in what you might think is not that big of a deal, but for them is a huge deal, because they're getting to spend time with you. They're getting to learn something they never knew before, and they're getting a chance to practice. What a great environment—a safe environment—for them to learn and grow in leading. It's hugely powerful.

Be A Mentor

One of the best ways to learn how to be a leader is to lead. When you bring someone with you and start investing in them, you're stepping into a mentor role. As you're being mentored and developing yourself, it's important that you take on that mentor responsibility for someone else, which will, in turn, raise your own leadership abilities as well.

I have talked about the need to have a mentor. I have talked about scheduling blank space. I have talked about the importance of being able to learn, read, and have the downtime. I've talked about investing in yourself and being able to bring someone alongside you. But this whole act of you being able to be a mentor closes that loop for leadership development. It allows you to pay it forward.

It can take work and patience, but it's totally gratifying. As you're mentoring someone, helping them own their ideas and solutions and all those things that you're doing as you're teaching them, you're leading by example, but you're also learning something every single time. No matter how scared you might be, no matter what your level of leadership might be, you're always going to learn something because the person you're mentoring will have a different perspective on things. Why? They're not you!

Whenever you teach something, you learn something.

You owe it to the person, to the organization, and to the team to be a mentor as well as a leader.

This touches back on some of the things I talked about earlier, especially developing those around you to the point that they can replace you. To be successful, you want to surround yourself with success. If you can mentor someone and pour into his or her life, you're giving the people around you the best opportunity to really perform at the level that you want to perform at yourself. That enhances your role, as well as the entire organization and that individual. You are paying it forward, not just for that one individual who needs your help, but also paying it forward by building a better version of you for the long haul.

Like I've said, the advantage of having a mentor is that you're working with someone who has been where you haven't gone yet, who's already walked that road. They've been where you're going. They've seen what you're about to experience. So, when I talk about the concept of paying it forward, and you flip that to being a mentor, you've been where someone hasn't been before, you've seen what they're about to experience.

First, you have to have a mentor before being a mentor. That's the whole student-teacher analogy. You can help someone else avoid some major pitfalls and obstacles that you experienced as a leader, but only if someone who has gone before you did the same.

Stay Sharp, Humble, and Hungry

One of the things that drive me the most is that moment when the person I'm mentoring "gets it." You see his or her energy level rise. You see that a-ha moment, that breakthrough second, where whatever I said and whatever I've done influences that person to finally get it. All of a sudden, things change for your mentee. He is doing things better than he's ever done them. He's doing them with more gusto than he's ever done before.

Being a mentor will make you a better version of yourself as you see the impact you're having on someone else, and that makes you want to be even better at mentoring and do more of it. When you see someone's eyes light up, when you see him or her able to connect the dots...that is so incredibly powerful. Quite honestly, it keeps you humble, because you realize how much you have left to learn. It keeps you hungry because when you see it, you realize you don't have all the answers yourself, and it keeps you sharp.

You don't get that if you're not investing in your leadership journey. You begin to get complacent and stagnant when you don't feel you have anything left to learn. I've seen a lot of great leaders over the years that allowed themselves to become complacent, because they quit investing in the people around them and themselves. They quit learning. They quit getting better. And that's a really dangerous place to be as a leader.

Stay sharp, humble, and hungry. If we can instill that in others and have that re-instilled in ourselves, we're well on our way to being great leaders and mentors, and doing incredible things!

Chapter 11

What Makes a Top Performer?

I've talked a lot about the things that leaders need to think about as they start working with their teams, and understanding the team dynamic is a very important part of that. I'm not talking about the function and formality of the team; I'm talking about the makeup of the individuals. You always have different types of people who come together in various arrays of activity to formulate the team, but how each one of those people show up is going to be a big determinate of how the bottom line is reached.

Every once in a while, you have a superstar. You have that person who just really steps up and shines. That person is more than a superstar—he or she is your high performer. This is the person who goes above and beyond. They do more, and they work smarter.

The One

It is a challenge for any business to have the right people in the right positions and to have people who have the potential to become those top performers. This doesn't have to be an exclusive club where just key people on the team have the ability to raise their performance level. You can have the majority of a team fall in this category, but the top performer I am talking about is that elite person, the one who catches the vision of the organization, who is able to devote themselves to becoming part of accomplishing that vision and see something that is bigger than themselves. They see the vision of the organization and latch onto it. They believe in it so strongly that it becomes a personal goal for them; they become an ambassador and evangelist for the vision.

At Chipotle, we talked about what being a top performer looked like all the time. This language permeated our culture, and it was awesome. We were all talking about the attributes of being a top performer while recognizing the individuality of someone who wanted to do more.

As we defined it at Chipotle, a top performer has the ability to elevate the people around them. They make the rest of the team better. As a matter of fact, they make the success of the team more important than their own personal success. This individual wants to make sure that members of the team are achieving their goals. It's about the team's overall performance and achievement as much as their own. It takes a lot of work and commitment to do this. It's not easy, which is why you are looking for the one who truly rises above the rest.

When someone is called a top performer in an organization, it means something. It can't be just the average employee who comes in every day and is doing a good job. It must be a person who's going to be able to elevate not only themselves but also everyone else around them for the betterment of the organization. They have to put forth a lot of effort and have the ability and skill level to be able to do the work and bring others along with them in their quest to achieve the goal.

When it comes to an average team member, of course, you want to help them develop skill sets and the mentality for the job. They need to know what is happening in their roles and why what they do is important for the next person, so they can better understand the big picture. But when you find the one with whom all this really clicks, that's the one you spend more time with, helping him understand how the performance of the player next to him also affects his performance. You want him to understand the team's dynamic, so he in turn, helps the person next to him become a better teammate. That's when you see change and higher performance for the entire team. This one person makes the success of the team a priority, and he also celebrates those same achievements with the team—as the team—and not just his own successes. Through a top performer's leadership, people around his become better. That's the goal. You don't want the person who carries the team on his shoulders. You want someone who's going to make the team a lot better as a whole.

My former CEO at Chipotle, Monty Moran, helped me define three key attributes: effort, ability, and desire. You can absolutely measure those three things in the work and life of a top performer. If you take away any of these three things, they can't be a top performer. You can have someone who has all the ability in the world, but if they're not willing to put forth the effort, they can't be a top performer. They are not going to elevate themselves or the people around them. If you have someone who is putting forth all the effort in the world but, despite trying, they just don't have the ability in this particular job, they can't be a top performer. It doesn't matter if you have someone who has all ability in the world if they don't have the desire to do excellent work; they're not a top performer. These three things are my baseline evaluation for if a person fits in the category of top performer or not.

Effort

Effort is the action someone puts into what they're doing. They're able to not only work hard but they're able to work smart. They're able to elevate themselves and the people around them. Effort is really energy and someone's ability to inspire the people around them. If a team is working alongside a person and see them putting forth that effort, taking pride in their work, and really working for the future, that will empower those watching. There are a lot of people out there working for themselves, trying to get ahead, but when you see them put forth that same effort in helping somebody else, that's special.

As people begin to get better in their roles and take on more responsibility, they can choose to be one of two things. They can continue on their own path alone and leave everyone behind, or they can choose to take a minute to slow down and bring others alongside them. That's what a leader (and top performer) does, and it's an important aspect of effort that isn't talked about enough.

You hear about people giving 115 percent, but that really means they are giving fifteen percent more energy than they actually have, so that is not really allowing them to be their best. I remember having a conversation in Dallas about this very thing in the context of a leader who had put forth the effort to do what they needed to do to bring someone alongside them, but that person wasn't interested. If you're working with someone, trying to elevate them, and they are simply not on board when you're doing all the work, you can't continue wanting them to succeed more than they do. All you're going to do is frustrate yourself and that other person.

It's different for every person, but I think when you reach the point when you realize you're the one driving the conversation, you're the one interacting, and you're the one who's doing all the work, you have to take your foot off the gas. You're probably working with the wrong individual, and they probably don't have the effort inside them to become that top performer I'm talking about.

Ability

Top performers have to function in their skill set, and that comes with training, development, and leadership. Typically, what I see within the ability category are people who have a natural skill set for a certain path, which goes back to talking about strengths. A person has to be working in their strength zones. They have to be able to execute.

People are only able to give their best when working in their strengths. When they have that ability and begin to be great in a role, it gives them more confidence and the ability to lead at a higher level. When operating in his or her strengths, a person functions with near perfect performance. That's the sweet spot with ability, and it becomes a hallmark of what others know about them. It inspires the people around them to try a little bit harder.

If people execute at an excellent level every day, that tends to be a result of the training they've received and the way they internalized that training. Practice—how they get really great in that skill—also leads to ability, and it really comes back to effort because the ability to execute at an excellent level has to come from the effort you're putting in. That's why there are times when a person has a natural ability, but he doesn't practice putting forth the effort. They're not able to execute it at an excellent level, even though they could—they've chosen not to. Ability is something that can be learned. So you can have effort and learn the ability through practice and training.

Desire

Desire is a want; it's an emotion. Unlike ability, it's not something you can teach. It's that internal craving, burning want, or belief that you can be better. It's the conviction that no matter what role you're in, there's always more to achieve than what you have in front of you. It's about getting better. I hate to see desire die in leaders when they get to a certain level and don't see anything more to accomplish. They kind of check the box when, in reality, top performers realize that you never arrive. The point of the journey you're on is to always move forward. You're never going to go back to where you were.

It's about charting new levels of performance—not only for themselves, but also for the people around them—no matter what position they might be in and no matter what level of success they might have already achieved. It's exciting to see other people you have poured into do well. That's an incredibly important component of being a top performer.

Sometimes you hear about desire compared to a fire. It's a burning, raging fire that you have to be able to move, but even fires need to be kindled. Sometimes you do see desires start to fall off. You see people who start out very passionate, but over time, that desire starts to wane a bit. They start to lost interest in the vision. They need that kindling, and kindling can sometimes be the people around you.

When that desire starts to fall off, it's typically because they have begun to rely more on themselves than they have on the people around them. If you see this happening to a top performer, it's important to sit down with that individual and say, *here's what I'm seeing.* Sometimes you have to help stoke that fire. It might be a new opportunity for that leader to get to a different level, but it's incredibly important as a leader to recognize when that desire begins to wane in a top performer. Sometimes, small wins are enough to light that spark of desire.

The top performer is going to realize that the point of departure is not to return.

It's incredibly powerful when you realize you should never again be where you are today. You should always be moving forward. If you perform at the same level next year as this year, you're only going to be doing a good job. You're not going to be excellent anymore, because the expectations are always going to rise—and they should. If the organization is healthy, the expectations should get higher every year, which means you have to raise your level of performance each year. If a person continues to perform at the same level every year, he or she will get passed over. It's always about reaching those new levels of performance.

The top performer is someone who performs at a very high level with high effort, high ability, and a burning desire. It's about his or her personal brand of leadership and how to inspire others along the way rather than shouldering all the work as individuals.

Effort, Ability, and Desire For Top Performers

Effort

- People who puts forth the effort to elevate themselves and the people around them in order to achieve the larger goal.
- They know it's not about them but about their personal brand of leadership.

Ability

- People who can execute skills at an excellent level on a consistent basis, day in and day out.
- Those who have the ability to do a great job and it becomes a hallmark of who they are, inspiring others to try a little harder.

Desire

- People who have a burning desire to get better, no matter what position they might be in or what level of success they have already achieved.
- If the point of the journey is not to arrive, the top performer realizes that the point of departure is not to return.

Chapter 12

Leadership Through Emotional Intelligence (EQ)

The topic of emotional intelligence (EQ) is a subject that isn't talked about much in the world of leadership and business, but it really should be, and I hope it will be more in the future.

There are four core competencies to emotional intelligence:

1. Self-Awareness
2. Self-Management
3. Social Awareness
4. Relationship Management

Daniel Goleman, the psychologist who helped popularize the idea of emotional intelligence, defines each of these areas:

1. *Self-Awareness*: knowing one's internal states, preferences, resources, and intuitions.

2. *Self-Management*: managing one's internal states, impulses, and resources.
3. *Social Awareness*: how people handle relationships and awareness of others' feelings, needs, and concerns.
4. *Relationship Management*: the skill or adeptness at inducing desirable responses in others.

When talent is evaluated, most people don't look through the lens of emotional intelligence. It's the hard skills they are looking at—the actual technical ability of a leader—and while that is definitely important, EQ is equally vital. Today, people are not leading very well in terms of emotional intelligence.

EQ is defined as a person's ability to empathize with other people—to be able to identify, evaluate, control, and express emotions. But that's just one part of it. It's also the ability to perceive and assess others' emotions and use those emotions to create structure, processes, strategy, and thinking for those people around you.

We can't get away from emotions. They're natural things, and how we react to certain situations, conversations, or even people who have different personalities can drive an emotional response. If you don't understand how your emotions play into a situation, how your team member's emotions play into their work, or are not able to spot those hot points, you can find yourself in a whole world of trouble.

You have to be able to regulate your emotions as a leader. Too often, we respond and react instead of taking a step back and counting to three or taking a deep breath and making sure that we respond thoughtfully. You can't be in a leadership position and allow your emotions to take control of the situation. Instead of emotions facilitating how you think through a problem, they can cloud the way you think through it if they're in control. EQ is the ability to use those emotions to really facilitate what it is you want to accomplish or what you want to come out of a conversation without letting them rule the situation.

Keeping a Level Head

It's not easy to do this, but you have to know where you are on the spectrum of EQ. You have to understand your own emotions and be able to manage and control those emotions to set the tone for everything else that happens down the line. If you can't go into something with a level head, you're going to also incite emotion from the other side.

How you show up emotionally will dictate, from start to finish, what happens in any situation.

You see coaches, bosses, leaders, or heads of teams who tend to lead from a point of high emotion—yelling, arguing, and demeaning their team members. You see those teams fall apart.

But then, you see a leader who comes in and offers the other style of emotion—care, love, and stability. Those teams buy into the mission better. If a hot-headed leader allows emotions to overpower the conversation, it may look like anger to the team. It may look like the leader is attacking a team member, or it comes across as overconfidence. Then when things start to die down, that leader may realize what he did and might even try to apologize for it, but what he's not doing is taking steps to get better for next time. He doesn't take steps to really respond differently the next time this situation arises. He doesn't understand this is a skill he must work on, or his employees will leave. We talked about this before: **people leave their boss, not their jobs**.

You can have people who are performing well in a role and who look good on paper, but from a leadership standpoint, they don't have the ability to grow an organization or develop a team because they're not leading with emotional intelligence.

How You Get There is as Important as Getting There

You can get the results, but *how* you get the results is just as important as simply getting them. You have to look at your emotions, and then you have to be able to evaluate and regulate those emotions. You have to recognize your own emotions as well as those of the people around you, because in the context of really getting to know your team and asking the right questions, you have to use emotional intelligence to help you dig deeper to ask the right questions.

If you try to come in and power through without looking at the emotional intelligence of yourself and the people around you, you're going to struggle and eventually fail. I think of organizations like a balance beam. On one side, you have emotional intelligence, and on the other side, you have a strong people culture, which is what you want. You want people who love working for you and want to do a great job. You want those top performers who really embrace your people culture. Yet, you have to have the emotional intelligence on the other side of that balance beam, because when you have those leaders who have the right level of emotional intelligence, that's what is going to help build the culture you need to drive results. Those leaders sit in the center of that balance beam and help achieve the balance every organization needs.

Sometimes leaders get so bottom-line driven that the emphasis is on the result, and they forget about how to get the result in the first place. You have to keep yourself in check here. Come back to that team, make sure the performance, growth, and life are still there, and the results will come. If you're off balance, you may not realize it right away. When you get results, but those results aren't reproducible or sustainable, that's a real problem. And, that usually happens because you dropped balance—the emotions of that organization are not regulated or recognized. You must look back and rebalance. Every organization goes through this, and you need to be able to tell when you're off balance so that you can get things back on track.

When you allow yourself to get on an emotional high, it's not sustainable or balanced, even though it might be a positive emotional experience. Eventually, that level is going to drop off, and you're not going to be able to reproduce that moment. There are times when you'll find yourself "in the zone." When you're in that zone, you can do some amazing things, but you can't expect that to be the normal, everyday occurrence. You have to have balance in place where you don't play too high, you don't play too low, but you find that spot where you're optimal. Play there. When you get into that "in the zone" moment, by all means, take advantage of it. Just understand that it's an anomaly and can't be reproduced every second of every day.

Raw Talent Isn't Enough

I've seen leaders who have all the potential in the world, ones with natural, raw talent that just needs to be developed and cultivated. If that leader is elevated to a position of leadership where they're impacting a lot of people, and they are counting on just raw talent, they're going to be like a bull in a china shop. They are going to make a lot of things happen, but none of them are going to be good in the long run. Things are going to break along the way.

The resulting environment does not allow the team to achieve the results in the right way. They're not going to be high-performing results, and they're certainly not going to be sustainable. The leadership landscape across every business and in every industry is littered with leaders who possess high levels of talent but never mastered the four competencies of emotional intelligence.

If you can't manage yourself—if you're not aware of how you are behaving when you're with your team and you can't manage those relationships—you are the bull in a china shop. You might be the leader, but you're not going to accomplish things the right way. I see people get removed from positions all the time, not because they didn't have a high level of talent, but because they did not have a high level of emotional intelligence,

When I specifically talk about self-management in the realm of emotional intelligence, I think it comes down to self-care. How are you caring for yourself as a leader? Are you getting enough rest? Are you eating well? Are you having an appropriate amount of downtime? Those things are all part of managing yourself. I've brought this up several times already, but self-care gets put on the back burner, and without it, you will find yourself trying to run on an empty tank.

When that self-management component is not in place, there's no chance you're going to have self-awareness, be able to manage relationships well, or be aware of how you behave socially in the context of the organization. That component is incredibly important, and it's what most leaders don't do well at all. It's the cornerstone to having everything else in place.

It's Time to Start Looking at Your Team's EQ

When it comes to hiring, you spend a lot of time looking at personality charts or skill sets and ability. You interview candidates and start to hear who they want to be and what they think they can do within the organization, but you don't spend a lot of time diving into EQ; yet, it's incredibly important.

HR departments everywhere have spent a lot of years and a great deal of money trying to develop excellent interview guides. These are awesome and super necessary to help gauge fit, technical ability, leadership abilities, and traits that are needed for certain roles. But you need to spend just as much time and effort measuring emotional intelligence. Not very many organizations do that well, and it's a missed opportunity. When you don't look at the emotional intelligence of potential leaders for your organization, you're inviting people into your family who could actually do a lot of damage. They might look great on paper, but in reality, it may be they don't have the ability to lead at all because no one took the time to develop their EQ.

The good news is there are some great tests out there that can be used for that, and they're not hard to administer. It's worth the time and effort to measure EQ in a candidate. HR Magazine talks about the three common ways to measure emotional intelligence: self-report, other-report (360 tests), and ability measures. The Bar-On EQ-i uses the self-report approach with a questionnaire of 133 items, which the participant is asked to score on a scale of one to five. Other reports use feedback from co-workers in a 360-assessment format. The commercial EI-360, created by the north American Institute for Health and Human Potential (IHHP), contains forty-seven statements for the participant and ten co-workers to rate on a seven-point scale.

That's how you can look past the raw talent of a candidate. Sometimes you get enamored with a personality or a resume, and you don't take the time to really dig deep and figure out what type of leader they are. I think you can only do that by looking at emotional intelligence.

Today more than ever, emotions play such a big role in how a person thinks and reacts in every aspect of their lives. With the advent of instantaneous social media, we're now able to express ourselves in a more open way. Let's face it, twenty years ago we weren't as emotionally driven as we are today, and I think that's only going to increase. Whether that's good or bad is not the issue—it's just the reality of today.

If organizations don't make looking at EQ a priority, we will see more and more issues within them. The companies that are moving forward today are the ones that understand a candidate's potential for success is based on more than just a skill set or motivation, but actually on her ability to get in touch with herself and those around her on the emotional level so that she can produce a higher result.

Chapter 13

High-Touch Versus High-Tech

We live in a world of technology, one in which everything can be automated. Every time you turn on the news, another organization is talking about how much more automated they're becoming. In this world of automation, it's important to look at how you approach that technology as a leader.

Technology is continually evolving and changing no matter what industry you are in, and it continues to become a part of organizational leadership. Technology is great for so many reasons. It allows for broad communication and getting the word out quicker about initiatives and things that need to be talked about, but I firmly believe it should accelerate the great things you are *already doing* without technology to develop existing and future leaders.

Technology as an Accelerator

In the context of leadership, I believe that technology should only really accelerate the great things you're already doing one-on-one and face-to-face with people. As great as technology is for the things it allows us to do, such as video conferencing, webcasts, and large presentations for a group of people who can't be in the same room with you, there's no way to replace **high touch leadership**, which is what I define as a more hands-on, shoulder-to-shoulder leadership style. You'll never convince me that's not the best way to lead. I think there are ways that you can use technology to help that along, particularly if you are trying to communicate to a large group of people all at once, but I don't think there is any substitute for in-person communication whenever you can make it happen.

There's also the real, practical application of technology when you train and onboard new employees. I think you need to make that as experiential as possible in terms of that hands-on training, while ensuring they're still comfortable with the technology. If you're teaching someone to take inventory, and you're trying to come up with the number for costs of goods sold, you can input all that information into a computer and get a number.

There's a huge value in helping them calculate that cost of goods number *without* the help of an inventory management program. Of course, technology can help you in terms of providing real-time information to help run the business more effectively, and that's a good thing. It just can't replace you and your team knowing how to calculate that information without the use of technology.

Don't rely too much on data as it's spit out. If you're not careful, you'll lose the art of instinct. You lose the opportunity to project and see things as they unfold, versus relying on a system to do the job for you.

A leader becomes lazy when they rely solely on technology.

You look at the report and the data in it, and if it looks good, it must be good. In reality, that's not the way the world works. There needs to be validation that what you're seeing on paper is actually what's happening.

If you're in charge of an organization, or any group of people, and you're in charge of certain metrics and key performance indicators for your business (which most leaders are), you get some sort of reporting weekly, monthly or quarterly. When you start to review those numbers, it's imperative to get out into the field and make sure that what you're seeing on paper is really what's happening. **The most important piece is the human connection, the people point.**

Technology is just a guidepost. It's a way for you to have the basic information so that you can get out there and validate that it's really true. And, when you, as a leader, get out there, you're able to look at how you can make things better. That only happens when you get out of the office and get into the field. I look at technology as dashboard reporting. It's super helpful, and it'll at least point you in the right direction. When you have that technology working for you, it helps point you towards the area that might need more of your leadership. However, the technology should not be doing the work for you.

People are the Engine

It's always good to be looking to grow technology and improve automation, but **you have to keep yourself balanced enough to realize that you still have a team of human beings that you're working with.** Think about it in terms of a car. You are going to need that engine to get you there, but you're also going to need the gas to go through the engine. You're going to have to use the accelerator to control the gasoline in the engine for you to get where you want to go. You can't get anywhere without the engine in your car. I view technology as being that accelerator to the business, but your people are the engine.

When a car is operating well, you can get in that car, go great distances, and even accomplish incredible feats, but that car needs repair and regular maintenance. When that happens, you don't just rely on a piece of technology to do it. Typically, you have to take it to a garage where there's a personal interaction between you and a mechanic, and that mechanic goes on to make that car better (along with the help of a little technology). You can leverage all the technology available in your industry to improve and enhance your leadership and get the most out of your teams and leaders. But in the end, there still needs to be that regular, hands-on maintenance.

Great people are needed to get anywhere as an organization. They are the most important factor in this equation. When you treat them that way, you begin to take time to personally invest in those leaders you're developing with that high touch approach. I don't think anything helps to calibrate hopes, dreams, and expectations more than being across the table from someone. When you look at the engine of a top performer, I don't think there's anything you can do better than to put care into that relationship, and that only happens from a high touch approach.

The great thing about technology is that it allows us to do more. It allows us to get off the phone. It allows you to get up from your desk, meet with people, and really invest in them personally. You don't necessarily have to spend time doing a lot of the menial administrative tasks because technology can get the information. Then you can get up and go out and, as I said before, validate that information by interacting with *real people* in a *real conversation.* It empowers you to do what you need to do to get out and be the engine in that company by being more intentional with one-on-one interactions.

Nothing takes care of the engine of a top performer better than the care you put into that relationship.

Balance the Investment

Technology platforms are being developed very quickly these days. I recently attended a restaurant conference, and the amount of new technology is unbelievable. From inventory management platforms to new hiring software to new training modules, new resources are added to the mix every day. It's important to continue developing and growing, but as you continue to develop and commit resources to create or implement those new technology platforms, you need to make sure you're devoting an equal amount of time and resources to creating platforms that will help you create future leaders.

A lot of that comes down to turning off your phone and sitting down with people. When I think about the most powerful interactions I've had over the years, they have come from me being in a restaurant, sitting down with the general manager, and being able to talk to him or her with no phone interruptions —really taking in the moment and my surroundings.

When you walk into the restaurant, you've got a lot of information on paper about the restaurant. You already know how it performs on paper. You already know what you've been told. But you get the opportunity to soak all that in when you are sitting down with the people in that restaurant. You get a chance to inspire them, but they get the opportunity to inspire you, too. With any visit, my intention is always to make a difference and leave part of myself with that team. What I realize more often than not is that I am taking part of them with me, as well.

You realize you need them more than they need you. That's what happens with great leadership. That's how you achieve the balance with technology; use that technology to get in there and have better conversations. It becomes a really inspiring place where you can see young leaders rise up. They're the future leaders of your organization, and you need them. They need you right now, but you're going need them more at some point.

As you adopt new technology and bring up new leaders, they are ingrained in the technology as it exists today, which already puts them just a little bit ahead of where you were when you started. You can see a natural progression leader after leader, generation after generation. As technology grows, leadership grows with it. You see a symbiotic relationship between the two, especially in today's world where everything is changing so fast.

Technology allows you to expand your influence and reach. It might be a video blog. It might be a talk that you record. You can narrow down those mediums used to communicate broadly into an opportunity to eventually have that personal, one-on-one conversation with somebody.

The bottom line is that technology is an important accelerator. People are the engine, and when both are applied properly balanced, you'll get the result that you want.

Chapter 14

Changing the Arc of Someone's Story

As you can most definitely tell by now, I truly think those face-to-face, one-on-one, shoulder-to-shoulder conversations have the largest impact on future leaders. I want to dive deep into this concept because it's the foundation of my leadership style.

I'm going to say something that is important. I really want you to hear and understand it.

A conversation can change a life.

I know this because it has happened to me. I can think back to a handful of conversations that changed the whole trajectory of my life from where I was heading to where I ended up. Those conversations changed the entire arc of my story.

You have a direction you're heading because of the choices you've made, how you grew up, or maybe even where you were born. Your story has an arc, and you may have never thought about your life as anything other than how it looks like it'll turn out.

An Investment of Time

What if someone took the time to invest in you—to sit down and explain options that you didn't even realized you had. Someone could have a conversation with you that could literally change that arc. Knowing something like that has the power to change your life's entire direction is incredible. I often think about the personal investment someone made in me as a young leader—because it did change my life.

When I joined Chipotle, I thought I was just taking a position. It sounded like a cool company, and I really did believe in the mission of changing the way the world thought about and ate fast food, but it changed my life in ways that I could never have predicted. I think about the move I made to Austin, Texas in 2005 or asking my wife to marry me in 1994. These were things that changed my life. I knew some of those decisions would bring life-changing effects, but I did not know about all of them. You never know when people might provide opportunities, or how a simple conversation could change everything for the person with whom you are talking. Yes, I wholeheartedly believe that an investment of time with just one conversation can change the arc of someone's story.

In the workplace, you'll see people who seem to be stuck in their arc. It could have to do with how they grew up or something that happened to them along their journey, but whatever it was forces them to keep that path. Sometimes, it's just a simple conversation that gives them the freedom to break through that glass ceiling. Those changes in their arc can mean a great deal in terms of how the rest of their story unfolds.

When I think about being put on that front counter on that rainy Thursday night in 1984, I can point to it as the moment where the arc began to change for me. It was just a small window of opportunity, but then it grew. And, that window began to open more and more and more, and that window became a door that I was able to walk through. I think about when I was told I could be a leader. I was fortunate to join an organization that really believed in developing their leaders, and I caught that vision.

It's the simple things you do for people that matter, the times you have no idea how much a small statement or affirmation can make that shift for someone. Leaders don't always fully understand the weight of the words they speak. A simple conversation in passing can inspire someone to change his or her story, and we may never fully realize that, which is a thing of beauty in leading well. This is why you should treat every interaction with every person you meet as sacred.

I saw a movie recently called *The Upside* that showcased what one conversation can do for someone. Kevin Hart plays Dell, a guy from the wrong side of the tracks and Bryan Cranston plays Phil, a paralyzed billionaire. In the movie, Dell was talking about how no one expected him to be anything other than what his dad was. But Phil started talking to him and told him that he felt Dell was smart. Dell laughed it off, and then Phil looked directly at him and said, "*No, you are intelligent.*"

It was obviously something that Dell had never heard before, and from the next scene on, you saw a huge change in who Dell felt he was. The arc of his life was forever changed. Phil saw and encouraged the potential in Dell, and it made a massive difference. Without giving the whole movie away, it's also a very good example of how much a leader learns from those he or she is leading.

What You Do Matters

I heard once that as a leader, our words weigh one thousand pounds, and I believe that is true. For you, what might be a simple conversation in passing can really inspire a person to change his life story. You may not realize that at the time. You may not have a lot of time with that individual. You may not have an opportunity to see how his story ends, but this is why I think you should treat every interaction with every person you meet as something to be revered—as a moment in time that you may not be able to capture again.

As a leader, there is likely no way you will ever be able to understand the impact you have on others' lives that you touch, but they will likely remember what was said to them. You can't understand the power of the seed that is planted or how that seed might grow with every subsequent conversation you have.

Whenever a leader comes alongside a person experiencing growth, they have an opportunity to fertilize that seed a little bit more each time they speak. Wherever you might be in the journey with that young leader you're working with, you need to realize that you have a chance to inspire change in someone. You have an opportunity to better someone's life. You have the opportunity to say something that's going to impact them in a positive direction. But just like you have that positive opportunity, it can very easily go in the other direction, as well. Keep that in the forefront of your mind. Keep the conversations positive and growth-related. Even when you address something negative, there's always a positive learning opportunity.

There is always opportunity for constructive criticism in leadership. The words that come out of your mouth will either affect someone positively or negatively. That's a big responsibility and one that comes with any level of leadership. Actions can speak louder than words. As a leader, what you do matters, as well. What you do can have as much impact on the people around you as what you say, so it's important that you think before you do.

In today's world, we tend to think what we do doesn't really matter. I think you need to get rid of that thinking. You need to realize that every opportunity has a chance to inspire someone and potentially change the arc of his or her story.

It always matters.

Blood: Water

Let me share an example of how one person or organization can affect change. I have some friends who run a non-profit in Nashville, Tennessee called Blood: Water (bloodwater.org). Their goal is to equip and come alongside African organizations as they work together to address the clean water and HIV/AIDS crisis in their communities. They do great work, and I've had the privilege of being able to work alongside them for a few years.

Notice that their goal is not to swoop in and try to get the problem solved before heading back to Nashville. They're putting in the hard work to labor alongside the existing heroes in those communities to help them build the infrastructure to get those issues solved and help them change the arc of their stories.

So, let's look at this in the context of leadership. This charity is literally extending life—giving someone the chance to have more years on this planet— to impact more people through their own lives. That's really powerful. As a leader, you have the chance to help people extend their leadership lives, extend their stories, or even change their stories completely. Your impact may be helping them invest in and develop more people. I think the impact we can have is grossly underestimated. You don't always think about the things you do as life-changing, and I think that's a miss, especially when we're talking about leadership. Whether you're leading a non-profit, a restaurant company, a church, or a family, what you do matters, and you have a chance to change the arc of the story.

With Blood: Water, one of the things that I love about them is they're constantly educating the people who donate money to their organization. They let them know they're changing the arc of the stories of those communities in Africa through their efforts. This non-profit wants people to know that what they're giving and what they're doing matters, even if they don't think it does. It doesn't matter how small the donation; it still matters. You can have that same impact as a leader. Everything you do matters. And so, the words you choose to speak, how you choose to invest in someone, how you choose to build someone up, how you choose to spend time with them. Whatever time you have with future leaders *will* change their lives. It's up to you if that is for the better.

Look at it in the context of what Blood: Water is doing. They don't just come in and solve all the problems, but they're partners. They work with the people, whether donor or recipient, in understanding that the relationship is what makes the difference. What a beautiful way to look at leadership: understanding that you're here to help, inspire, educate, encourage, and grow others. And as a new leader, when you're learning from a seasoned veteran, when you've got someone taking that time, the wealth of experience and knowledge that awaits you is unfathomable.

Challenge the Status Quo

Sometimes by changing the arc of a story, what you end up doing is changing the status quo and inspiring others to be more and do more. You're challenging them to do that. So let's talk about what that means and what that looks like.

I've cautioned you before about getting to a point when you feel like you've arrived. When a certain level of success is achieved and you feel like you've accomplished something great, it's easy to rest on those laurels; that's a human thing to do. But when you have a culture that continues to inspire, challenge, and focus on developing people, you realize you can inspire greatness in others, which, in turn, should inspire you to keep challenging things.

When you realize in the context of how you live your life, run your business, and raise your family, that what was good before (maybe last year or last month), is no longer good enough, it's like throwing gasoline on the fire. It's the moment you realize that what was done to inspire you to that higher-level performance is exactly what you need to do for those who you are in charge of leading. And that has you continuing to challenge the status quo.

You don't allow yourself to rest on the prior level of success you've achieved, because you realize that you've created something that you can't stop.

In the best years I was at Chipotle, when we were developing people and opening new stores, I remember standing up in front of a thousand people telling them, "We could not stop this if we wanted to." We didn't want to, of course, but we couldn't have, because we had invested so heavily in our team. We had invested so heavily in our leadership—and we had invested heavily in their leadership—that it created this kind of revolution in which everyone was always going to get better. We realized that no matter how good the results might've been before, they weren't going to be good enough with our increased expectations, and so that desire to make things better is what really inspired us. You inspire others to be more, to do more. You continue to raise your personal level of leadership as a leader, and that's how you challenge the status quo.

People talk about losing momentum, but if you think about it, momentum doesn't really stop. Sometimes it changes directions. Or it may slow down, but it doesn't really stop. If you're not challenging the status quo, you're going to see that momentum go the other direction, and you'll actually start falling behind. As leaders, we want to lead and be out front. You want to constantly be moving in a forward direction, building that momentum up, bringing those leaders behind you so that they catch that momentum and can ride the wave.

Think about surfing. The idea is not to be on top of the wave. It's to be in front of the wave. As a surfer sees that wave coming, they try to get right at the peak and ride the wave in. If they're not catching it on top (if they're not getting to the point where they're challenging that status quo), they lose the wave. The wave moves on, and that surfer finds herself in the still water waiting for the next one. You have to build momentum, not just build momentum to progressively grow a company or an organization, but to propel the other leaders you're working with forward.

Jim Collins uses the flywheel analogy in *Good to Great*. It's a very heavy wheel, and when running a company, you have an incredibly large goal that can be heavy, too. You keep pushing and pushing until that wheel begins to turn itself and starts to build its own momentum, but your job is to make sure that momentum is going in the right direction. If you do things in your organization that are not true to the vision or things that damage the culture, that flywheel will start spinning in the other direction and take on a life of its own. But if everyone is pushing in the same direction towards the things you want and need to accomplish, they're going to happen naturally. If you go the other direction, you're never going to be able to do that. In fact, you may find yourself spinning right into irrelevance.

Never forget that what was done to inspire you to a higher level of performance is exactly what you need to do for those you are leading. You need to get everybody on board, moving in the same direction—the right direction—creating that energy, creating that movement and that motion, and then you are truly affecting company culture and changing the arc of the story.

Chapter 15

Why a Leadership Culture Matters

When we're talking about culture in terms of leadership, we're talking about something bigger than just growing an organization or business or just growing a leader. I'm talking about a much deeper concept here. This is about the environment—a way of life. I'm talking about building a natural order and the impact a single leader can have on an entire culture.

I took over Texas for Chipotle in 2005. I was coming into a market that was struggling. They had really lost their way and their voice. The momentum in Texas had definitely shifted. I didn't know anyone on the team of existing staff, and I knew that would be challenging. Everyone told me how difficult it would be, and they weren't wrong. It was. But can you guess how I started? With a simple, one-on-one conversation conducted with every existing leader. I let them know I was there to support them, and they were more important than whatever the results were at the time. I told them I wanted to build a relationship with them. I was determined to build a positive leadership culture in these thirty-five restaurants spread out over Houston and Austin.

Two Paths

When leaders go into that type of a situation, they think one of two things. They either think they can't make a difference and just try to maintain the current status quo, or they realize they're going to really need to invest by rolling up their sleeves and getting in the middle of the mix to make a difference.

It's a choice of two paths—one leads to serving themselves, and the other leads to serving other people. I chose the latter. I tried to come into the situation as more than a boss. I came in as the leader who was willing to invest and believe in the team members and the organization. When a leader helps the team believe in the organization, those beliefs are what create the culture, the way of doing business, the system, the process, and the core values.

I defined leadership earlier as influence, and leaders impact their organizations through their personal influence. One person can have a huge impact, but it's all about creating belief and using the beliefs you create to create the culture you want.

If you choose the selfish thought of serving yourself, it may put you on a bigger pedestal, but overall, it's not going to get the culture you want it. That team is not going to follow or be inspired by selfishness. When you serve others, they start to understand you are there for them, you've got their best interests at heart, they're more than just a number to you, and the end result is a culmination of everyone's efforts. That's when they start to buy in to your plan. It's powerful to sit back and think about the impact you can have on an entire culture by simply choosing to invest.

The Right Culture

You want the culture to be going in the right direction, so make sure that everything you do is building towards a positive result.

You must show yourself to be trustworthy
before people will trust you.

You can build trust by being willing to be a part of the hands-on work, not just the overall, high-level strategy. When I first got to Texas, we had a lot of individual leaders who were running around trying to be in charge, instead of a team of leaders trying to figure out how they could help each other be better leaders.

You have to realize your actions have consequences, and whether you're the leader of the overall organization, your individual team, or yourself, every decision you make impacts the culture of that organization and has far-reaching impact beyond what you realize. Much like talking about the investment you make in people, you don't always realize how your investment in culture will pay off. When you build a culture that is not healthy—not empowering—it also does more damage than you can possibly know.

Culture is something that you do. It is built by the words you speak, the actions you take, and how you steward that leadership. Remember, I mentioned earlier that leadership is stewardship. It's temporary. You are accountable for the results that you get. You're not going to lead in this position forever, so you need to realize that everything you do in the organization either helps reinforce that culture or helps tear it down. Make sure you are creating the culture you want, one that is going to deliver the type of results needed. You dictate the right kind of culture in the organization through your actions and the words you speak, making sure everything lines up with the core values that you say you have.

One bad apple can spoil the whole bunch, and that's very true with culture. You have to constantly make sure that you're getting the right people trained in the right direction. Get them indoctrinated with the cultural standards that have been set. If an environment of toxicity comes in, it can taint everything that you've built up to that point, and then it becomes a struggle to get things back on track. I've seen multiple organizations and companies suffer when they build the correct culture, but through change in leadership or a breakdown in process or systems, the culture is thrown off a little bit and things start to unravel.

You see a company that's been doing great for five, ten, or even twenty years, and then for whatever reason, they start to fade away. In some cases, they ultimately cease to exist, because they've not protected that culture the way they should. **You're only as good as your most recent success**—your culture is only as strong as the last person you promoted. What got you here will not keep you here. You have to constantly look at yourself when it comes to personal performance. You have to be willing to reinvent yourself. That's also true of organizational performance. The expectations are always getting higher, and you have to think about the people that you surround yourself with and whom you bring into the organization. They have to be able to support the culture that you want.

Organizational leaders have to keep this in mind, because you can very quickly find that you've lost that edge of culture—what made you special—and you have to guard against that.

Long-Term Results

In terms of biology, the word culture is defined as the conditions that are suitable for growth. When I think about a culture of leadership and the conditions that are suitable for growth, they have to start with surrounding yourself with the right caliber of leaders to build a culture you want. It has to start with you. You have to be the type of leader who can build that company culture, but you have to surround yourself with others to help you.

That culture can look like a lot of different things. It can look like a culture of hospitality. It can look like a culture of excellence. It can look like a culture of compassion. It can look like a culture of leadership development. All of those cultures (and others) will be directly reflected by the people who you surround yourself with as a leader—both now and in the future.

It's easy to lose sight of the future. You tend to think about the here and now, but you need to be thinking about what the culture of the organization will look like in three, five, or ten years. Are you making the right decisions to protect and cultivate that culture that you want to see built? Are you making the right decisions about those you are bringing into the organization now, so you have the infrastructure to support future culture? It requires much intentionality to think through those questions when you build your team, talk about talent management, and discuss succession planning. When you look at what your future needs are, they'll be based around your key business drivers and your operational and strategic plans. You have to ensure that your bench strength will support those future growth plans. In order to get that long-term result, you must start surrounding yourself with the right people.

You should be continually looking for people who you can add to the puzzle, and that search needs to start within the organization. It's not just looking to bring people into the organization. Look internally for those who are in positions now who you can elevate, promote, and grow to that next step, because they already understand the culture that you're in and can move it forward naturally. I've always focused on trying to promote from within, because I think that really gives you your best opportunity to preserve that culture. When you have people who already know your organization, your mission, your vision, and they've lived it, that's really powerful.

Of course, everyone starts as an outsider at some point, right? I've been the new guy. You've been the new person. But my general rule of thumb is that when you choose to bring someone from the outside into your organization, you do so because they are the right fit for your culture. I want to bring someone in because I want to, not because I have to. It's really critical that you're bringing in the right people into your organization, especially if you're a high-growth organization, and you just can't sustain promoting from within to fill every position. That's perfectly fine, and that happens, especially if you have a short runway to get to where you need to be.

Bring people in who understand the culture. Remember, you're not just trying to fill the position. That's an important distinction when you bring someone in from the outside. Every person who you bring into your organization from the outside who hasn't grown up in that culture will have a bit of a learning curve. Make sure they're able to understand how you want them to contribute in the right ways to get the results you want them to get. I'm all about protecting that culture. I don't want to put someone in a position and then regret it later, because they don't understand the culture.

When you make sure the conditions are right for growth,
then you have the conditions for that right culture.

Generational Differences

With every generation, the previous generation worries about the next. We worry about what's going to happen when these kids grow up. You have to realize that as generations grow, they grow with a slightly different understanding of the way the world works than the previous generation—new technology, new thought processes, new ways of doing things. They're indoctrinated and ingrained in their world. It's a natural thing that needs to be dealt with in every organization. There comes a time to meet in the middle, when you allow your culture to evolve to be able to accept some of the ideas, challenges, and ways of the new generation that is coming up. You can do that without losing the dexterity of the culture or the core values that you've created.

I've said it before, leaders are learners, and one of the best ways to learn is to surround yourself with people who might have a different view than you do. When talking about the generational shift and building the right team that can get results, I think it's incredibly important you have a diverse group of people at the table. It's okay to have viewpoints that aren't the same. Conversations should happen around what is important to the Millennial generation (or the next generation coming up) versus what might be important to someone from a generation or two before that. It's okay to be inclusive of people who have different views than our own, and that includes people who have a different view of leadership, as long as their core values are in line with yours. It's incredibly empowering when you do that because it keeps your organization fresh and current. You never want to get stagnant and trapped by old thinking.

You tend to surround yourself with people who are like you, but that's not always the best thing for your culture. When it comes to building a strong culture, it's important to surround yourself with people who will challenge you. That's part of how you then challenge the status quo.

Culture never stays as we build it. It's like everything else. How you communicate changes over the years. How you operate changes over the years. Yes, the core values and the core strengths are foundational, and if you build the culture in the right way, everything else will come into play and shift year after year, generation after generation. If you never lose sight of the core values, the culture will continue to grow.

Chapter 16

What a Leadership Opportunity Looks Like

Opportunities come from all different angles and directions. Leadership opportunities show themselves from unexpected places and in unexpected ways, as well. If you're not careful, or if you're unaware, it's easy to miss some good leadership moments and opportunities.

When a young leader is trying to lead for the very first time, or they're in a new environment trying to lead, they're usually looking for an opportunity to shine. They need to recognize the opportunity in that moment. That is the time for them to lead.

Opportunity is simply a set of circumstances that line up and allow someone to lead.

As a leader, you have to recognize that opportunity doesn't necessarily come gift-wrapped, shouting, "Oh, this is the moment!" Instead, you need to lead well in every moment and realize that each of those moments is an opportunity to make an impact.

We miss too many opportunities, because we're looking for the perfect time, place, or situation, so it's important that you are keenly aware of the opportunities that are literally all around you every single day. They can be big or small, but taking advantage of those opportunities is about you contributing at a higher level to the team you are leading when a circumstance shows itself. For me and countless other leaders, sometimes those circumstances show themselves as a result of someone seeing something in us; they thought we were capable of making an impact, so they pushed us to do so.

Creating a Set of Circumstances

In the earliest days of building the team at Chipotle, we developed an internal career fair process where we invited longtime employees to sit down and have a conversation about how they wanted to grow their careers. These employees would be people who exhibited all the characteristics that I've talked about throughout this book. They were our top performers who had given us effort, shown their abilities, and obviously had a desire to do more. They were fairly nervous but so proud to have been invited. They dressed up and came in for an interview, thrilled to have the opportunity to talk about their accomplishments, what they were doing in the restaurant, and how they thought they could contribute more.

The leadership team members were the ones who really benefited, because we saw the future of the company in these employees. We knew that we were on the forefront of something really special. From this one circumstance of being invited to this career fair, these employees—these future leaders—were allowed to get in front of us and share their stories. They saw the circumstance come their way and were able to recognize and seize that opportunity.

Through that opportunity, we found they had more bandwidth—more under the hood—than we might have thought. It all comes back to the same thing I have been drilling into you this entire book. We learned that information about them by sitting down with them face-to-face, engaging with them, and asking questions. We created the opportunity. We created the circumstance for them to grow as a leader, but they are the ones who made the most of the opportunity. We simply gave them an audience.

We intentionally planned the opportunity for them, but sometimes opportunities come our way that aren't planned. Somebody might leave an organization, or maybe someone decides to step away from leadership. When those unexpected circumstances arise, it creates an opportunity that, as leaders, you must be able to recognize.

However it happens, whether intentional, as a part of development, or you are simply in a position where you're next in line for what you've been working towards, just know that the opportunity might come when you least expect it.

This can happen for anyone on a team. Let's say you have a new team member who might be younger or inexperienced. Maybe this is her first job, and she is struggling. I love to see a more experienced team member, without provocation or being told to do so, stepping up and helping that newbie. That's taking real initiative, and those opportunities come up on a daily basis no matter who someone is on the team. Those little moments lead to bigger opportunities because they are empowering not only the new guy or gal but also the senior team member.

I have a policy of, whenever possible, never do a task alone.

I love to see a longtime employee who has skill and some proven results see something in a new hire that they know can be developed, and then recognize they can influence the new kid on the block.

In the restaurant world, it could be a task as simple as counting the inventory to make a prep sheet for what's needed to get through dinner. Instead of taking that prep sheet, going into the cooler, and knocking it all out yourself, it's choosing to take someone with you. Bring them into the walk-in and have them help you count. Walk them through what is needed to prepare for dinner. You know you could do it yourself in fifteen minutes, and it will take thirty minutes to bring them along and get them up to speed. Those fifteen minutes that you spend with that individual could light a fire in them, because you're giving them an opportunity to lead—to learn. They're going to put their name on that prep sheet; they're going to say they helped decide how much was needed to prep for dinner to make sure the team had enough for service.

That's creating a leadership opportunity for both people. Leadership opportunities come in all forms, shapes, and sizes, and they're just moments—preconceived or on the fly—that give you and others the opportunity to step into a leadership role.

Creating Leadership Opportunities for Others

You might see leadership ability in people who just don't see it in themselves, but you have an opportunity here to set the stage and let them know they are leadership material, to tell them they have the ability and should investigate it. That is certainly part of my story.

One of my favorite inspirational quotes is: "I'm a leader today because someone told me I could be." I don't think you can convince someone he is a leader if he doesn't believe it, but you *can* create the opportunity for him. But do be careful not to push too hard. When you push too hard and try to prove to them they are a leader, you end up wanting it more for them than they do for themselves. If they're hesitant or don't buy into it, you need to move on and focus on those who do want it. There's a balance between creating an opportunity for people, being able to ask the right questions to draw the desire out of them, and trying to convince them that they can actually be a leader.

For me, I was all in! I was so excited that Brenda saw potential in me. As a young crewmember at McDonald's, my boss told me I could be a leader, and I chose to embrace it to the fullest. I stepped up into that role, and that little bit of encouragement is why I'm writing this book today. How could she ever have known just how far that wee bit of support would take me?

I was cleaning my office the other day. I keep almost everything, so it was not a menial task. Let's put it this way: I have performance reviews from the 1980's. I have always kept my performance reviews, because I think they're important and a part of my legacy. So as I was cleaning, I was reading a document from September 1986 after I'd just attended my first management class. I had just graduated from high school the previous spring. I was a young, eighteen-year-old kid who didn't know anything, which is probably what saved me. The fact that my owner operator believed in me backs up everything that I have been talking about. The investments my leaders made in me really paid off. They made me who I am today.

My managers had no idea how I was going to respond to them telling me I could be a good leader. I'm certainly not the only one who was given opportunities, but how many lives were impacted because they saw something in us that we didn't see in ourselves? Their belief in me resonated with me. It was something I needed in my life at that time, and that moment has led to this career.

My growth from that moment multiplied exponentially. Fast-forward two decades, and I was sitting in a meeting when one of our human resources associates made a passing comment about an internal career fair platform. I latched onto it immediately, knowing I needed something like that. I had just taken over the Texas stores for Chipotle, and I needed a way to cultivate the talent that I knew I had but had not been unearthed. I was coming into a situation in which we were underperforming, and I was there to invest in my team to make sure we turned it around.

Once I heard the internal career fair idea, my wheels started turning. I don't think I heard anything else for the rest of the meeting. I thought this was the way to engage with people and help them see something in themselves that they hadn't seen yet. It was at that moment I realized what had been done for me, I could now do as a leader across a lot of restaurants, and that was really exciting.

There are a lot of those moments, ones I won't forget in my journey. Two decades in, there was one particular moment that brought everything full circle. I got on a plane and flew to Houston to meet with my team. I remember telling them what we were going to do, and while I had no idea what it was going to look like because we had no material to support it, I didn't have any doubt that the internal career fair was what we needed. I just had to figure out how we would build it out.

We began providing a high level of leadership and coaching to our restaurant teams. We were very intentional in growing young leaders to expand their influence. Recognizing talent and then doing something to help a young leader begin to expand their influence is the key to opening the doors to opportunities beyond their wildest dreams.

That idea was fifteen years ago, and it's as true and important today as it was then. It's those moments in our life that create a ripple effect that can be seen for many years to come. Sometimes it takes a while for that ripple to reach the shore, but it always does, and it always comes back. You always have an opportunity to lean into what happened in your life to influence someone else in theirs. It's that little circle of what it means to be a leader. As you create leadership opportunities, they're going to be reproduced and sustainable over years and years and years.

Chapter 17

Don't Burn the Ships to Secure Success

B urn the Ships" is a phrase that came from the story of Hernán Cortés. In 1519, Cortés set sail to Veracruz, Mexico with his crew. Upon arrival, Cortés' made history by destroying his ships. Cortez had the men burn their ships, sending a very clear message to his team—there would be no turning back.

I remember reading this story for the first time, not thinking of it as a leadership story, but it really is. There are some people and stories that inspire you, and then there are others who show you what you wouldn't want to do. While I love the story of Cortés and his exploration, when I think about him landing in Veracruz where he was about to begin his great conquest, I see that he didn't trust the people he had with him. He had all this passion and was ready to go do what he needed to do, but he was so afraid that his team would side with the enemy that he made absolutely sure there was no way for them to escape. They couldn't leave.

In reality, and especially in today's world, you can't make someone do something if they don't want to do it. The goal is to build a culture, a company, and an organization in which everyone *wants* to stay. They *want* to be a part of something amazing, and you can create something amazing with a team of top performers. That team can drive those results and develop more great people who will carry your vision to the next generation of leaders in your organization.

In other words, if you have to burn the ships,
you may have the wrong team.

I hear Cortés's story, and I wonder if the story would have been altered if he had a different crew. Maybe if he had more loyal people (or if he was more loyal and invested in and developed his people better) he wouldn't have had to burn the ships. It's an interesting story of the journey of leadership, showing that if you try to lead through fear—if it's always about you—you're going to end up with a lot of people who really don't want to be there. Then you may, in fact, have to burn the ships when you realize that it's either you or them. Then, the leadership becomes the problem.

What a lesson to be learned from the story of bringing a group of people along with you and then putting them in a situation where they have no choice but to do the things you want them to do. That doesn't build the right environment for success. It may succeed, or it may not, but it builds a *function* rather than taking the time to build a *team* the right way. Finding the people who *want* to follow. Leadership is not getting people to do what you want them to do, but getting people to a point where they want to do the things you need them to do. It starts with getting the right people who buy into the mission.

Get the Right People

It starts with making sure *you* are clear on the vision and exactly what it is you want to do. History tells us that the story of Cortés could definitely have gone better if he was clearer—what exactly was the mission and how clear was he when he cast that vision? It's imperative that you know those objectives when leading.

I heard someone once say, "I feel like I'm saying the same thing over and over and over and over again. I'm just tired of saying it."

The person on the other side of the conversation said, "Good, you're halfway there."

You've got to continue to preach the vision. Make it portable; make it memorable. When people know what the end game and the results you want to achieve are, it's much easier for them to rally. It's also easier for them to decide if this is something they want to be a part of. If you're clear on the vision, it's going to be much simpler for you to identify talent and for that talent to identify whether or not they want to be with you.

A great idea is only a great idea if there are great people around you to make it happen.

You won't have to burn the ships if you have great people around you who want to be there. When you have the right people, define a very clear vision, and articulate that vision well, you get people to buy into doing something special for the completion of that vision, not just because you need them to do it. This goes back to something we talked about in an earlier chapter: not making it about you or your wants or desires but putting it back on the team to create something incredible.

To keep that vision moving forward, you will want to make sure there's a clear path towards success. That could mean removing obstacles, which may include a low performer.

Sometimes there's a person on the team who's just not the right fit. Over the years, there will be someone on the team who the organization has simply passed by. You are not able to coach them up, and they don't have the ability to elevate themselves or those around them. Keeping a low performer on the team will prevent you from attracting the top talent that you need to help accomplish your goals and objectives. It will cause a top performer to leave. Top performers don't want to work around people who aren't going to do their best to contribute to the success of the organization. One of the biggest obstacles to team development is when you have someone on the team who doesn't want to be there, no one else wants them there, but the leader doesn't remove them.

It always has to start with human capital. It has to start with the team. Do you have all the right people there? If you don't, what's the right thing to do for the integrity of the team? The right thing to do first is coach the low performer up, but if you find that you can't, you have to be able to remove them so the rest of the team can thrive.

A team is not very different from any other machine. If one tooth of one gear is not working properly, it can throw the whole operation off-kilter. You want to make sure that all the members on your team are reaching their peak, and that can't be done with someone on the team who doesn't want to be there.

I want to be clear about this: a low performer is not someone who is just a little bit different than your highest performer. It's someone who is not performing, who doesn't buy into the vision, who's not putting forth 100 percent. I'm not saying you have to have only the best in the world on your team, but you have to have people who are willing to put all the effort they can into accomplishing what you're trying to accomplish.

You're not always going to have the best people in the world on your team, but you should have people who you know will put forth the effort, ability, and desire, to get to that level at some point. They're going to be in a position where they can contribute at the highest possible level. Remember, you can coach ability and effort, but you can't create desire where there is none.

You must know what it is you are going after and have a roadmap that leads the way when people want to be a part of something amazing; they want to feel like they're contributing to something in a way that's going to be special. They want to know how to get there. They want to know what they're working for matters. Don't let a low performer on the team keep you from attracting top talent or cause your top performers to leave.

I have a friend named Paige Chenault who is the CEO and Founder of a nonprofit called The Birthday Party Project. She has a mission to bring joy to children living in homelessness or transitional living facilities through the magic of birthday parties. I met Paige years ago on a flight coming home from a leadership event that we had both attended.

It was clear to me after that two-hour flight that she was incredibly passionate about her idea of building an organization that, at the time, served homeless children in the Dallas/Fort Worth area. She was a professional party planner and was planning her own daughter's birthday party when she read an article that made her think about homeless children and how they didn't get to have one of those big parties.

It ignited a passion within her to figure out how to help solve that problem. She believes that joy changes lives, and a joyful community can change the world. These celebrations are a chance for kids to dream big. The parties her organization throws are so much more than a celebration; they are a loud exclamation point that these kids matter.

Early on, she struggled with getting the right people around her—people who were really committed to the overall vision. Over the last few years, I've seen her vision grow to Detroit, Minneapolis, San Francisco, Kansas City, Chicago, Atlanta, New York, D.C., and more. All along the way, she's had challenges trying to build and scale an organization.

She knew it would take teams to host these magical birthday parties, and The Birthday Party Project is what it is today because of the passionate team of people she's built. She calls her party coordinators "heroes." They are volunteers who rock the parties every month all around the country. Her board members are committed to the health of the mission, and her team digs deep to support those efforts around the country.

She realized failure was not an option. She only wanted people around her who wanted to be there, so she got really clear on her vision. She surrounds herself with leaders who challenge her to be better. She has created a culture of accountability that keeps everyone honest about where the organization is headed. She doesn't have to burn ships because she is assembling a team of people who share the vision and want to be a part of it.

It's a beautiful story, and it just goes to show that I'm not only talking about building out a giant restaurant chain or Fortune 500 company. These principles can certainly be applied to those larger organizations, but they can also apply for a party planner with an idea to use her strengths to better someone else's life. No matter where you are, if there's something you're doing that you're passionate about, that you know is going to make someone else's life better because you can do it on a bigger scale, it's worth the effort. It's worth putting the right team in place to help you. Paige's story encapsulates everything I've been talking about. Paige doesn't necessarily have to be the business driver. She has the vision, and she can get the right people around her to help drive the business. I think oftentimes the opportunity to do something on a grander scale is missed. There are things bigger than you are, and you've got to find the right team to help you make those things happen.

We started this chapter talking about Cortés and how he burned his ships to motivate his team to push forward on his goal, but in the reality of today's world, that doesn't work, nor is it possible. The goal is to build a culture in which everyone wants to stay and be a part of something amazing. The way to do that is to build a team of top performers to drive results and develop more great people who will carry your vision to the next generation of leaders in your organization, who are beyond your reach, so that you don't have to burn those ships in order to get results.

Chapter 18

Asking the Right Questions

I started working with Matt, my boss at Chipotle, back in 2002, and we worked together in varying roles for the better part of a decade. He was the master of asking questions he already knew the answer to, but he never made you feel dumb when he asked. You knew he probably already knew the answer, but you also recognized that he was genuinely seeking your opinion. He wanted to know what *your* thoughts about the question.

That relationship inspired me to always strive to find the right questions to ask as I developed my leadership skills. There's a difference between good questions and those that just aren't helpful—the ones that are not going to build anyone up or encourage them. You need to be asking the right questions.

When you ask the right questions, you're illuminating the darkness, confusion, and uncertainty in the minds of the people you're leading. When you ask the right questions, you invite clarity, action, and discovery at a whole new level.

What Seems to be Happening Here?

When you walk into a room, a restaurant, or an organization, you have to figure out what is happening. You have to be clear on the root cause of an issue and be able to diagnose that. Don't just look at the symptoms of whatever problems you see.

For instance, if I walk into a restaurant and see a dirty lobby manned by a team who isn't smiling or a filthy dining room with trash overflowing, it's easy to look at those things and say, "Wow, we have a real problem here."

What you need to be able to recognize is that those typically aren't the real problems but symptoms of the bigger problem. You've got to use the symptoms you see to help you diagnose the root cause of the issue. At Chipotle, we all learned how to use the symptoms of a situation to diagnose the root cause, and it was so powerful for us.

You have to be able to see and understand all the dynamics you are dealing with. Until you totally understand the full scope of the situation, you're not going to be able to make the necessary improvements, and asking the right questions in these situations prevents you from jumping the gun. It's easy to go in, see a situation, and immediately want to implement a fix. The problem is that you don't always know the *right* fix until you can get to the root of the issue. Asking *what seems to be happening* gives you time to sit back and investigate. Get as much information as you can about why things appear the way they do. Then, you can fix that leaky valve—seal it off—and turn things the right direction.

You have to be able to immerse yourself into a situation and become part of the solution.

Approaching a situation with an "it's not my problem" perspective is never helpful. **If you're the leader, it is your problem.** It's incredibly powerful when leaders immerse themselves in a problem and own it right along with the rest of the team. People are going to be much less defensive in that situation. A great leader understands they're accountable for everything that's happening on the team and refuse to deflect the accountability.

What Does This Make Possible?

After you're clear on what or where the leaky valve is and have gone in and made some adjustments, think about what you can do to help your organization become even better as a result of dealing with that situation. A great leader views problems as possibilities to become an even stronger organization. They look at a challenge and see a possibility to become a better leader.

Great leaders help their team realize that while things might not be great today, they do control tomorrow. The way they impact tomorrow is by asking *what does this make possible?* What does this issue make possible? What does this new competitor coming into your space make possible? Always have them look at a situation or obstacle from a perspective of what can be done to be even better in the future. It's incredibly empowering for a leader to ask that question of his or her team.

As you're uncovering things, figuring out why things are happening or what's actually happening, you'll find the right moments to ask that question. There are no failures, only learning points. There are no mistakes or accidents, only times for changes in direction. I've often seen that when something is uncovered within an organization and I've gotten to the root cause, that's when those magic moments of something new are found. Something may have looked like a mistake to begin with, but it then opened the doors to create or do something better because it was found. That's the way a company or an organization gets stronger—when they can figure out what things challenges make possible.

What Are We Going to Do About It?

The natural evolution of the above question is *what are we going to do about it*? When you create a truly cooperative environment in which your team can fully engage with you as the leader, it creates synergy across the entire organization to develop multiple potential solutions for addressing a problem that needs to be solved. When you engage with your team and open an honest dialog, you will have empowered your team members in ways that other organizations only dream about. You're involving your team in finding a solution to the problem and, as a result, they will own that solution.

That's why the question is worded the way it is: what are *we* going to do about it? This isn't just you deciding. Yes, you may have the final say, but to get there, you're going to ask your team *what are we doing about it*?

It's not good to swoop in and diagnose the root cause of an issue and jump right to *what this makes possible*. They don't need the leader to save them. That gives no thought to the future, because it would not have been approached from a standpoint of *what are we going to do about it*? The team would not own whatever the solution might be.

You must create a truly cooperative environment in which your team can fully engage with you to develop solutions to the problem that needs to be solved. Make sure you get buy-in from the team for the plan you all decide upon follow moving forward, and then, you're off to the races.

What Are We Learning?

Every problem, every situation, everything that happens provides a teaching moment. Not everyone will ask this question, but as the leader, you've got to ask the question:

What are we learning from this and what are we going to do differently moving forward?

When you take the time to unpack the details surrounding a problem and how you chose to resolve it, it allows you to plan for future issues that may arise. For this reason, you may see obstacles sooner than when they'd normally appear on the radar.

In the restaurant space, I learned this over and over again. It could be something about rolling out a new menu item. It's been tried in the kitchen and works great, but maybe it was not tried in a select couple of restaurants before it was rolled out everywhere. When you do a large roll-out involving every restaurant, where not every team is the same and equipment could be a little bit different, you end up with something that can't be executed to the highest possible level. You and your team have to learn from those experiences. This is true of any initiative. A program can look great on paper, but it's important to learn from every misstep, so your team can come alongside one another to help plan for future issues in similar situations. What are you learning about it to make you, your team, and your organization that much better through this situation or obstacle?

You must see that every problem provides a teaching moment. The people who are closest to the action are going to be the ones with the best perspective on what needs to be done. When you're asking the right questions, you also need to make sure that you're asking the *right people* those questions. It's incredibly important as a leader to make sure you've gone to where the action is and you're not asking people who don't have good perspective of the problem or the potentially great things you want to do in the future.

Asking the right questions of the right people produces the right answers. Your insight will be greatly enhanced on every specific situation, and you and your team will find the best solutions to each and every problem. Remember, leadership is less about controlling your team and more about leveraging every opportunity to build a team that can control itself. Whether you're an individual, small organization, or large organization, asking the right (four) questions is how you do just that.

Four Powerful Questions

What seems to be happening here? —Getting to the root cause of the issue.

What does that make possible? —Making sure you're putting that plan in place to grow from this.

What are you doing about it? —Take action to get people engaged to move forward.

What are you learning? —To make you, your team, and/or your organization that much better through the situation or obstacle.

Chapter 19

Diagnosing the Root Cause

How do we get to the reason behind why things are the way they are? When things don't go smoothly, you always want to know why that is. What caused it? How can that mistake or issue be avoided or what can be done to keep that from happening again? Regardless of how exactly you ask, the question of why is something that should be investigated from multiple angles rather than only to discover what went wrong. Let's dive in and unpack the idea of finding the root cause.

When you look at the root of an onion, the intact root is what keeps the onion from falling apart. So, when thinking about what's causing someone to perform poorly, you think about there being something in that root that is coming apart. To really be able to understand what's going on when you see performances that don't happen the way they should, you have to understand that what you're seeing on the surface is not always the whole story. You can meet someone, and it seems like things are going well, but that's because you haven't taken the time to actually dig down and see what's happening underneath the facade. That's also true for bad performance. What you see is often not the full story.

Understanding Bad Performance

You must be able to diagnose the root cause of a low performer. When doing so, there are some questions to ask:

1. Do they know the standard?
2. Do they care?
3. Do they have an unenlightened leader?

You start by asking: Do they really know the expectations and standards, and do they even care if they're performing at a high level? If the answer to those two questions is yes, then the next place you have to look is leadership. Do they have an unenlightened person leading the team who is not providing them with direction? This is where you start to really understand the full breadth of what's happening. When a person seems to be under performing, it may not be him causing the problem at all. It might be his leader who's creating the issues.

It's your responsibility to make sure your team knows the standard, whether it's what they're supposed to do, how they're supposed to do it, or what the expectations are. When it comes to caring as a leader, you can instill a sense of excitement or a sense of urgency. You can get people to buy into the vision if you position it the right way. So even if they come in thinking it's just a job, with the right leadership, you can draw people into caring about the overall mission.

You have to evaluate your own role in the answers to the above questions. You have to do a gut check. When you find an answer that you wish was different, you have to look internally into the processes and leadership. Have they been trained properly? Through business and all elements of life, it's easy to point to someone else not performing at the level that you wish they would, but you must start evaluating your own role in it. Are you leading by example? Your role is to help them understand the right way to do things, so the first question has to be: what is my role in this? Have I done everything I needed to do?

If you haven't done everything you can do as a leader to help people succeed, then you have not done your job. At some point in that conversation, you have to start evaluating your role in the process before you can tag people with the label of a low performer. They may indeed be low performers, but you've got to work your way through the process before coming to that conclusion.

Don't dump low performer labels on team members or, worse yet, let people go, without knowing if it's really their fault. I've let people go and watched them go on to join another team and be phenomenal. That showed me that the problem wasn't with that performer; that problem was internal.

Understanding Great Performance

Too often the focus is put on negative performance—it's just human nature. The tendency is to want to make things better, so the focus is put on *what's wrong*. Leaders are taught to improve performance. They always want things to be better. That's a good thing, but leaders don't take enough time to really understand what great performance is. You're taught early in your career to look for what's broken and ask if it can be improved upon.

Everyone has an experience that reflects a culture of excellence. If you think about this in terms of a great restaurant visit or retail experience you've had, you find you're caught up in the feelgood moment, but few people think about whether they understand *why* it was excellent.

The more time spent focusing on what is working and why it's working, the more often you can reproduce those results.

I've learned how to ask better questions in order to better understand how team members were able to perform at such a high level. When you take the time to go in and ask people questions like, "Why was this experience so great? Why was that level of service you provided so amazing for that store? Why does the food taste so on point today?" you're going to find that people are going to be more than happy to tell you exactly why they were able to perform at that high level. When you find a culture of excellence, and you really take the time to understand why it's working well, it almost always involves the manager giving away credit to the team members: "It was this person today who made salsa. It was this person today who was on the register. It was this person today who was working on the line."

This is just another example of wanting more for others than they want for themselves, which is the fuel for being able to sustain great and repeatable performance. This also inspires confidence in the teams you're working with and helps them go out there and do it again.

When you look at the root cause of a problem, you're looking to eliminate. But elimination does not always equal moving forward. Sometimes, it's taking a step backwards. When you're looking at what's going right and why that's happening, you want to reproduce it, which gives energy, movement, and motion forward. That is an enlightened way to look at things. Instead of looking to eliminate or fix, how can you reproduce what's great? How can you do that over, and over, and over? I'd love for you to get to a place where looking for excellence—and how to reproduce it—becomes the norm for leadership, and by doing so, problems just disappear.

Culture of Excellence

You can get information from looking at both sides—understanding why there's poor performance and looking at great performance—for positive information about what can be reproduced. The combination allows you unbelievable insight into what you can do for future success. You want to use this information in such a way that you get the most out of everyone involved, including yourself, and create a culture of excellence along the way.

There was a shift that happened about halfway through my career at Chipotle when there was a lot of talk about a culture of empowerment. We wanted to create high-performing teams and started to recognize the best performers. We looked at how to elevate those leaders to positions where they could have more influence than they currently did. Questions were asked of our top performing GMs (General Managers), and we learned from them. Through that process, we began to understand why things were working in their individual restaurants—what they were doing, what type of processes were in place which their teams were able to execute, and what made things so great for them.

We started to understand the root cause of that goodness, instead of the root cause of problems. We were able to celebrate and reward those results, but more importantly, we were able to

create more confidence in those high-performing teams to reproduce those results in other people, at an even a higher level than
they were able to perform by themselves. That's important because
when you think about your own performance, your own livelihood,
and how you're viewed, you start to think about how you're able to
get those results at an even higher level through other people. And
that leads to surrounding yourself with people who are even better
than you are. You're able to develop, coach, and lead.

This is how you make an impact.

This is how you build a culture of excellence.

This is how you develop people at the highest possible level,
and this is what allows you to build a culture that's almost bulletproof because everyone becomes a champion of that culture. Everyone begins to think more of the people around them than they do
about themselves. Everyone is pulling for each other's success. By
looking at root cause, whether root cause for poor performance or
root cause for great performance, you can start to figure out what's
making this thing tick—what's making it work—and how you can
reproduce it in an ongoing, ever-evolving process.

---

*It requires a conscious shift in the mind of the leader to look
at things differently.*

You do have to look at more of the half-full glass versus the
half-empty glass. You have to spend as much time (if not more
time) looking at the results you're getting, the ones your teams
are proud of, and the results of people who are performing at high
levels as you diagnose the root cause of problems.

When you understand why things are working well, that will
give you really valuable insight into some of those problems you

might be experiencing in certain parts of the business. You then have a unique perspective on how to go in and coach some of those problems with insight from the things you've experienced that are going well, which I think is the real magic there.

In a restaurant, you are always looking at the numbers. You've got to hit those numbers. You've got to hit those marks. And that's fine, but you have to read between the numbers, too. Yes, you're going to have benchmarks, but when you look between those numbers, that's where you really start to see performance on an individual basis. That's where you can start to rely on what I am talking about here—understanding the root cause of greatness and understanding the root cause of bad performance—to make sure those numbers aren't just being hit but exceeded.

I've emphasized throughout the book that *how* you get numbers or results is just as important as getting them. In order for you to really be skilled in your role, in order for you to truly achieve notable results, in order for your team to be great, you have to get those results in a way that is not only sustainable but is repeatable. That's when the culture you have supports the results you're achieving. It's not smoke and mirrors; it's not one good month; it's not one good quarter. There is an ongoing culture of high performance in your business. Those are the results you want. You want that ongoing success that just seems to happen because you've built a culture of excellence based on the root causes of both successes and problems.

Chapter 20

Why Vulnerability in Leadership Matters

This chapter is about something that doesn't get mentioned often in leadership. Leaders are always seen as the strong ones—those out front, the ones directing—but the role of vulnerability in a leader is very important, as well.

The last chapter talked about creating a culture in which people want more for each other than they want for themselves. In order to get that culture where you're creating sustainable, repeatable results, you must show that you're willing to let your guard down. You have to be vulnerable, which means you own your part of the equation. If there is a results deficit, you own it. This isn't being vulnerable in a way that is weak. This is being honest. This is being really authentic, and when you are willing to share that information and show your wounds, you're better positioned to communicate throughout the organization, whether it's one restaurant, one market, or an entire organization.

Better Communication

You're better able to communicate the vision with more passion, candor, and emotion, which will also give more clarity to the team. A key aspect for leadership is communicating with clarity, because you've immersed yourself in the details, you're leading by example, and you've made a personal commitment to the work that needs to be done. So it's not just asking your team to do more. It's leading by example. Vulnerability in leadership allows you to become a much better communicator.

The biggest impact on great communication is becoming a great listener. If you don't allow yourself to accept information from someone else, communication becomes a one-way street, and you'll never get that true, authentic response from the person with whom you're communicating. Vulnerability allows us to receive that communication in a way that pushes us deeper into what needs to be fixed or further into understanding great performance or poor performance. Then, we know what should be reproduced or what needs to be adjusted.

When you're communicating just to tell your side of the story, there is no connection.

Oftentimes, people are communicating without connecting, and when that happens, a wall is put up on the other side of the conversation. People crave connections in today's society. There has never been a better time to look at how big a role vulnerability plays for an enlightened leader.

Vulnerability allows you to open yourself up for this duality in communication. You can be a strong leader. You can be who you're supposed to be in a leadership role and still let the team leader you are working with know that you are in this together. You're pulling in the same direction. Yes, you have different roles, but when those roles play out as they should, you're going to get to a great result—together. Vulnerability and the partnership it can lead to really does create that culture that allows you to excel as a leader and communicate incredibly clearly, especially when you're worried about the person on the other side of the conversation more than yourself.

Authenticity Rules

Vulnerability is not something that can be faked. You're not pretending to care. You're not pretending to listen. You're actually getting to a point where your authenticity shows through. You're authentically vulnerable, open, and willing to listen and accept what the other person is saying.

Many years ago, I took over the Florida region of the market for Chipotle. I remember meeting with the leadership team for the first time. This was after I'd spent a couple of days at restaurants, and it was time to come back together and discuss. We were all in a room and everyone desperately wanted to hear my thoughts, but I wanted their thoughts. I led the conversation in a way where they had to answer my questions. They're the ones who were closest to the action. I was new to the market and this team. I certainly had opinions, and I was going to share those, but I needed them to share first. They did a great job without even really knowing what I was trying to pull out of them. They were able to clearly expose everything that I wanted to say myself.

We had a log jam. We just couldn't seem to develop enough people for this region. And to be honest, it was because of some of the leadership that was in the room. It was because of some of the people that were already in leadership positions. I remember making the statement:

"If you can't develop people, you can't work here anymore."

When I said that, you could almost feel the air in the room being sucked right out, but when they wrapped their heads around my statement, they realized I was right. In the years since, I've had many people in that room tell me that was a pivotal moment for them in their careers. All because I had to be real and authentic with them. When you have an authenticity rules mindset, your leadership will shine through.

No matter how magnetic or charismatic you might be as a leader, and we've all seen or had those leaders, you have to remember that authenticity is king. People see through bravado.

That conversation with the Florida Chipotle leaders even inspired me. I knew I had addressed the elephant in the room, so then it became *what am I going to do about it*? I decided to lead by example. I made a personal commitment to the work that needed to be done. That's something that will always inspire others and make them rally around whatever the goal objective is for leadership. Some leaders will never achieve their full potential because they're not allowing themselves to be vulnerable enough to lead at an authentic level.

Authenticity also protects you as a leader. The people you are leading will see through someone who is not being authentic. In my experience, the people who are following may not even know someone is the leader yet, but through that person's authenticity, others buy into their message. When others choose to buy into a story, they are naturally drawn to the more authentic person. Not everyone knows how to get there, but they do want that authenticity on some innate level. They want to learn more about it. The magic happens when they start to model that behavior and figure out how to unlock that equation for themselves. And it looks different for everyone. You don't want a bunch of carbon copy leaders because that's not authentic. When everyone can internalize what it means to be an authentic leader, that's when an amazing culture is born. Leaders who lead with authenticity and are honest about every aspect of the business, about what they themselves can do better, and about what needs to be done, it will inspire everyone around them to accomplish the goal.

The ability to be authentic enhances the leader as much as it does anyone else. Now, as someone who is being authentic, you don't have to follow a mold or pretend to be something that you're not. You can bring your own personality into it. You can bring your own feelings and thoughts. You're not just liberating your team members anymore; you're liberating yourself to be the best leader you can be, because you're showing up in a real way.

I think of this in terms of my own life as a leader. I've seen other leaders who have gotten it over and over again. Authenticity allows you to lead without worrying about what everyone thinks. It allows you to lead in a way that's truly focused on the mission. When you lead from that vantage point, even when you're having a conversation that's not pleasant or about an issue or opportunity that you know needs to be addressed as an organization, the authenticity is indisputable. The other person in the conversation may not like it. They may not even think you're right, but because you're leading from such an authentic level, they will pause and take note of what you're saying and internalize it. They might even figure out, "Okay, what do I need to do with this? How can I make this better?"

When you're truly an authentic leader, it opens doors to communication that you would have never had if you had not built that level of trust. It's a level of trust that will only continue to grow as you lead by example. You're not trying to hide anything. You're not trying to mask anything. You're not trying to make something seem better or worse than it is. You're truly leading from an authentic point of view as a leader. You're not worried about how people are going to take the message in terms of how they view you. You just want to get the message out there, and you're doing it in such a real and vulnerable way that people are compelled to listen.

Telling Your Story

When you're able to lead from a point of authenticity, you earn the right to tell your story. I think it's really the best part of your leadership. It's not always easy, but you'll get comfortable with being able to share your story. When you tell that story—with all the details—to someone one-on-one, the newest leader in a restaurant, or even the newest employee, you're making a connection that you would not be able to make any other way. It's very relational. I've done this so many times over the years— sit down and share my story. Sometimes it's been one-on-one; sometimes in a big group setting. When you lead from that authentic point of view, from a place of vulnerability, it allows you to tell your story openly.

Your story is going to inspire someone else's story.

It's going to light a fire in someone else, or it may cause a fire that's already inside of them to grow. Never underestimate the power of the connection made when you sit down and share some of your scars. It's going to inspire others to talk about their leadership journeys openly, too. It's happened to me over the years. It doesn't take a long conversation with me to know that I have a little bit of a stutter. It used to be profoundly worse, but the stutter gives me a platform on which to tell the story about the investment that was made in me years ago. It also gives me a platform to talk about how I've addressed the stutter over the years, and how I've worked to manage it.

For the most part, no one is telling you that you have to tell your story at work. I'm telling you that you absolutely should, because it allows you to open doors that you'd never be able to unlock otherwise. Everyone has a story. By the way, this is not about marketing. This is the art of telling the story. When you're able to share that throughout your organization, it will inspire others to do the same, and that continues to work toward establishing that repeatable culture I've been talking about.

Our stories are always different. No one has lived my life, in my shoes, exactly as I've lived it. But there are intersecting points that all of us cross. When you as the leader are willing to use your journey to enhance someone else's journey, it allows the person with whom you're working align themselves in such a way that they start to think, "Hey, this person is like me in a lot of ways, and if he can do this, I can do this."

It gives you the chance to express, "I was just like you, and I am just like you."

They see that they put their pants on one leg at a time, just like you. They see that you go through tough things in life. Even though your life and theirs look different, they start to see the similarities in things that have happened, the inspirational moments. It's those flash points that make the little differences in your life and that they see can make the difference in theirs, too. You inspire teams by showing them they can align themselves with you. We can all learn something from each other. We all have a chance to take a little something from everyone we've met, and I think that's a really beautiful thing.

This allows people to relate to you in a way they otherwise wouldn't have been able to. It will cause them to be more open with you. Those conversations will start to unearth things that are really helpful, things you're able to help them address in their journey very early in the process.

If you can help draw out that vulnerability—that story—at an early point in people's leadership journeys, and they learn how to incorporate that into their lives, you've taken time, (sometimes months or years) off their journeys to leadership in terms of the impact they can have. So when you take the time to share that level of vulnerability with them, they turn around and do the same thing with another person down the line. It's a domino effect.

The Art of the Question

I am coming back to this topic because I want to talk about how vulnerability plays into mastering the art of the question. There is such power in the questions you ask leaders. You can ask a question that could absolutely shut a conversation down, or you can ask a question that gets way more of an answer than you thought you'd ever get. When you're seeking to understand what your team thinks about an idea, or if you want to get their input, the right questions are going to build loyalty, trust, and a *can-do* attitude quicker than anything else.

These are not the questions that you already know the answer to. You're asking these questions from the perspective of being an authentic leader who is willing to show vulnerability. You really want to hear their opinion. You really want them to weigh in on the conversation. People want to be heard. People want to have a seat at the table, and this puts the art of the question in a whole new light.

People are going to quickly answer your questions, and they're going to own those answers. That's what I mean by helping create that *can-do* attitude faster than anything else. It's also going to earn loyalty and trust because you took the time to sit with them. You asked them. You incorporated their feedback into your final decision-making process.

What I've learned over the years is that the people who are closest to the action are the ones who have the best instincts about the direction the company should go.

They may not know all the intimate details, and they may not know how everything is structured, but they don't need to understand all that. They just need to be able to share their gut level instincts about the direction and initiatives that are being planned.

That's when being vulnerable is so powerful, because you've made them feel important through the process—because they are important. You have to take the time to sit with those young leaders and ask those questions, so they can weigh in on the ideas that you have. This is what helps build the allegiance you need in an organization.

When you do this, it's time to put on your big boy or girl pants because when you open up these kinds of questions to those people who are in the grind, and you honestly want their opinion, you will get both positive and negative feedback. You really have to bring strength of character when you open up these kinds of questions, because you're asking for people's thoughts and opinions based on their experiences, and you may not get the answers you want.

But you're likely going to get the answers you need.

The ability to accept the negative feedback takes not just vulnerability but also a little bit of strength and courage, as well.

You have to take it one step further and ask yourself, "Okay, now that I've been exposed to this information, what am I doing to do about it?"

It's not just a two-way communication. It's two-way communication twice. You're asking the question; you're getting feedback. Then you're going to have to deliver on what you're going to do with that feedback, and then they're going to respond with how well it went. Many years ago, I was told, "Bobby, when you ask the question, you have to be prepared to deal with the answer you get." So it's really a two-way street there—twice.

Lead by Example

How you seek that information and how you accept that information are important, because others will watch you. When you take the time to sit down and ask the question, it says a lot to the group of people you're trying to communicate with. It shows humility. It shows that you're authentic as a leader. It shows that you're willing to be vulnerable, and it shows you are able to lead by example, because you actually showed up to have that conversation. You showed up to ask those questions. You showed up to figure out what you and the team could do to be better.

One thing I hope this book does is show you that being a vulnerable leader is not a sign of weakness but a sign of strength. It allows you to have staying power to influence real organizational change. It's not easy to be vulnerable and let your guard down. I don't want to paint the picture that being a vulnerable leader is easy to do. It's not. That's why you don't see it very much in leadership. Everyone has the ability to be vulnerable, but they don't because it's mistakenly viewed as a sign of weakness. It takes guts to show your authentic self and be honest about shortcomings, but it gives you huge opportunities to show what you're doing to improve.

And as I've talked about, that will inspire others in your organization to do the same when they're honest about who helped them thrive and get to the position of leadership they're in now. That inspires people to want to be that inspiration to others. It will inspire them to want to rally around young leaders and mentor them. It will inspire them to want to develop that next generation of leaders. And when all those things happen in concert, it creates an opportunity for everyone on the team to leverage their strengths and make everyone around them better. All because that leader chose to lead by example, show up, and be vulnerable as a leader.

That's why vulnerability in leadership matters.

Vulnerability might be the greatest strength a leader can have, because it invites other people in. It allows them to see you show up in an authentic way, and it opens up communication in a deeper, stronger, and more profound direction. It allows acceptance of all the insight, faults, opinions, and judgments in a non-critical manner so that you can use that information to produce this ongoing result—a culture of excellence.

When you show that vulnerability in leadership, it isn't a sign of weakness but of strength. You have the staying power to influence real organizational change. I think about organizational leadership a lot, I look at companies that really model this well, and I see them thriving. I want every leader who reads this book to understand that vulnerability is a true sign of strength and when done the right way and with the right coaching, it can allow you to achieve much more as a leader than you ever thought possible.

Chapter 21

Beware of the Unenlightened Leader

Shift moments are instances when you start to align yourself with a thought or a scenario that really makes you think about what you're doing and, more importantly, how you're doing it. That's what I hope has happened as you've been reading *Cutting Onions*. I've talked about the unenlightened leader throughout the book, but this is something that must be talked about in-depth, because it is part of the foundation of my leadership philosophy. **Unenlightened** is defined as having or showing a lack of necessary knowledge or understanding and failing to impart that knowledge or understanding.

Everyone knows how important leadership is to the long-term health of any organization but *knowing* how important leadership is won't be enough to help an organization accomplish its goals. You must also *be* a great leader who creates a culture that supports the organization and the future. In order to be a great leader, you have to surround yourself with people who are as good or better than you. That's what enlightened leaders do. Unenlightened leaders do just the opposite.

The concept of unenlightened leaders first came to me more than a dozen years ago. I remember having this light bulb moment when I realized what the concept was all about. I had just taken over a market for Chipotle where everything was out of sorts. I had met some great people, and a few of them were struggling. What made this situation so tricky to sort out was that in almost every case, the people I had been told were great by outgoing leadership were actually low performers, and the people I had been told were low performers were actually quite good. The light bulb moment happened while I was driving around Houston with my founder and CEO, Steve Ells. He used the phrase *unenlightened leadership* and defined an unenlightened leader as someone who is afraid to surround themselves with people who are as good or better than they are. This was so powerful for me that I've never forgotten it, and it has become a big part of my leadership philosophy.

At best, an unenlightened leader is not going to be able to lead at a high enough level to be able to get the results they want. At worst, both he and his entire team could be set on a course for destruction when they operate from an unenlightened state of leadership.

Operating from Fear

Unenlightened leaders who operate from a place of fear would rather keep people around who will not challenge them, strive to be better, or make the people around them better. It feeds a need for control, ego, and superiority, which will destroy an organization if left unchecked.

Unenlightened leaders won't arm a team with all the information they need. They'll never get to a point where they're building trust in their team. The team will pick up on that, and it will drive them not to follow the direction or do things up to the level of excellence that they normally would. Unenlightened leaders can convince themselves that they are in a state of enlightenment and are doing the right thing by holding on to information. It gives them a sense of power and control, when, in reality, it does just the reverse. Their team likely won't understand the direction they're headed, and that makes it incredibly dangerous because they are operating blindly in unchartered waters.

You want to operate from a position of confidence. When you do, your team will respond to your strength and perform better because of it. You'll be able to cultivate talent, which is empowering for your team.

We have all seen leaders who operate from a position of fear, when you know they're holding something back. But operating from a position of fear really limits you and your team. It keeps you from finding those star performers who not only promote better work from the team itself but can also support better work from you as the leader. This gives you the opportunity to learn from those you've brought in and promote yourself, because you've got a great support system. Operating from fear is detrimental to both the team and you. You should be raising your level of performance as you bring in people around you.

This reminds me of a time during my career at McDonald's. My manager was great and gave me a lot of things to do. I felt like I was growing in my career, and I was eventually going to get a shot at a promotion, maybe even running my own restaurant someday. I was excited about that. It was only after I did get promoted, which was about eighteen months after I thought I probably should have been, that I found out what happened. It turns out I was working for an unenlightened leader who was operating from a place of fear. In this case, she was afraid someone was going to take me away from her if she empowered or elevated me.

When she went to her meetings and talked about staffing and succession planning, I was never on the list of people to get promoted, because she was so afraid that I might get moved from her restaurant. That's another way that un-enlightenment shows up. She wanted to keep me inside her scope of control. If she was working from a position of confidence, I would have been promoted sooner and had more opportunities for growth, supporting her in the process.

Threatened by Top Talent

What that manager did with me is the next level of un-enlightenment in leadership. She didn't mean to, but she accidentally brought someone who was better than she was. Sometimes someone slips through the cracks (in a good way), and you get someone who is really good. But an unenlightened leader feels threatened by that top talent. Low performers make the unenlightened leader feel better about himself. The unenlightened leader will purposely look for talent they know could never be as good or better than they are—who don't have real potential to grow their career. By doing so, they feel like they will always be the leader.

Instead of embracing good talent and thinking about how you can help develop this person, ego becomes more important than excellence. It feeds the need to feel secure, but it will destroy a team—and eventually an organization—if it's not addressed. If an unenlightened leader accidentally brings in someone with high talent level who should be cultivated and developed, typically that person gets ignored. That top talent will wind up going to another organization where they can find a leader who will develop them and help them grow. This is a problem I see in a lot of organizations. It's incredibly important to identify this and address it immediately when you see it happening in an organization.

Ego becomes more important than excellence when the person in charge just loves being in charge, regardless of what the bottom line or overall performance looks like. It will bring down not only the performance of the team but could literally squash any kind of growth or crush any kind of opportunity for superior work.

People can only go as far as the leader is allowing them to go. If that leader is unenlightened, they're not going to get very far.

And there is such risk in allowing that top talent to leave your organization. If they are capable of great things, and you let them slip by you, they could go on to do great things for another organization. They could be contributing to your organization, but because you had a person in position who was threatened by that top talent, you never get to see any of their potential contributions play out. That's a huge business risk.

Don't Let Mediocrity Be the Best You Can Achieve

Unenlightened leadership never allows you or your team to excel past mediocrity, and mediocrity breeds mediocrity.

Don't let mediocrity be the best you can achieve.

The definition for mediocre is *of only moderate quality, not very good*. When mediocre is the best you can deliver, that in and of itself is a problem. But if you are an unenlightened leader creating a culture in which you have a mediocre expectation for performance and a mediocre execution against your key initiatives, that's only going to breed more mediocrity.

When you have that kind of culture, no one feels like they have the power to create change—the power to challenge the status quo I talked about earlier. Excellence is not an option. Even if you do have someone remaining in the organization who has the ability to become a top performer, they don't feel like they have the power to change the organization because of the culture of mediocrity. When you have a mediocre performance culture, you never really get to address the root cause of the issues. You spend your time fighting fires and never move an organization to a higher level of performance, because you're stuck in a mediocre loop that is the best you can achieve.

That is such a dangerous place to be. It's easy to see how an unenlightened leader will breed an unenlightened team. That's where organizations really start to fall apart, because that second-tier performance is going to ultimately affect the end result. And it doesn't just lower the expectations of ourselves; it increases the chances of losing top talent who find their way to another organization and out of the company entirely.

I hope this chapter makes you feel a little uncomfortable. This is not where I want you to stay. If you are here, you can still become an enlightened leader. And even if you are not an unenlightened leader, I hope reading about them shows the weight of what it would be like to be in that position or to have someone in that position within your organization.

A team can fall into hopelessness when an unenlightened leader leads it, and top talent can sniff that out. They may not be able to tell in the interview, but they will certainly be able to tell pretty quickly on the job if their direct report is unenlightened.

If you are reading this and find that you are operating from a place of fear, if you're afraid to bring others around you because you may lose something in the long-term, if you're putting your success above the company's or team's success, if you're threatened by top talent, if you're afraid to bring people in who will challenge you or who are better than you, you might just be an unenlightened leader. If you are okay with mediocrity, if you're comfortable where you are and you don't want to get to that next level because it means more work, you're operating from a position of an unenlightened leader.

Let me challenge you to ask what would happen if you were to upend everything you're doing now? If you chose to operate from a place of confidence rather than from a place of fear? If you weren't threatened by top talent but chose to really embrace them? If you realized that the mediocrity in the organization is not going to get you where you know you ultimately need to go? What would it look like to start creating a culture of excellence? Making these changes—choosing to become an enlightened leader—could literally change both your destiny and the destiny of your team.

Chapter 22

Embrace the Enlightened Leader

I had to talk about un-enlightenment because it is real, and it is out there, but now it's time to talk about enlightened leadership. An enlightened leader is a well-informed leader with a modern way of thinking. An enlightened leader can see things that others can't see. They see beauty where others might see damaged goods. They see the potential for excellence where others might skip over that new hire. When you open up your point of view to live out a culture of excellence, you are operating from a more enlightened perspective and are able to achieve top performance from both yourself and your team.

When the word enlighten is defined as a verb, it means *to give (someone) greater knowledge and understanding about a subject or situation.* As a leader, you go out and you gather information. As you go to make a decision for your organization, team, or department, you do so with extreme clarity and focus on what's best for the organization. You know that what got you here won't get you where you want to go, so you're always looking for ways to make things better for tomorrow. And your team will see that.

Enlightened leaders fully understand leadership is not about them and bringing in talented employees who can make everyone around them better, including the leader, is what allows an organization to thrive, not just survive. An enlightened leader realizes that tenure doesn't always equal excellence and developing future leaders means building a culture of leadership development that is sustainable and reproducible, which is the key to long-term success.

When we put an emphasis on hiring the best people, ensure they are trained properly, and allow them to work in their strengths zones, we cultivate a culture of excellence that raises the bar of performance for everyone on the team, and that will help ensure the efforts put towards leadership development will have an amazing return on investment. In fact, Gallup research shows that people who get to use their strengths every day are six times more engaged in their jobs than those who don't.

Create a Culture of Excellence

When ego is eliminated, the selfish veil of un-enlightenment is removed from your eyes, which allows you to see things other than your own effort, your own standards. This is when you can make a shift and build the environment where tomorrow can constantly be improved over today. It must be an ultimate realization that you're only going to be able to achieve the best you can achieve by having the best people around you at all times. You start to see all the things that could be, can be, or will be because you're now going to pour into your team. I've often heard it said that **leadership isn't taught; it's caught**. That is absolutely true.

It's something I have experienced while consulting on a number of occasions, and it's such a joy to see. There was a time when I came into a legacy organization that had been around for twenty-six years. They had just been through a very difficult transition where the outgoing leader certainly had some influence in the organization, but the transition could have gone better. I came in with a fresh pair of eyes and a pair of hands ready to get in there and work.

When I caught the vision, it was my job to help the team do the same and see things they hadn't seen before. I was able to help them get really clear on who we wanted to be when we grew up and what the endgame was. It was a great example of seeing how what got them to that point wasn't going to get them to the future. We instituted a culture of excellence by putting an emphasis on hiring the very best people, training them properly, and allowing them to work in their strength zones—allowing them to use their strengths every single day. You'd think that would be intuitive, something every organization would do naturally, but it's not.

Without a commitment to invest in the people culture, no organization will be able to fully achieve what they want to achieve. There may be some short-term wins and some level of success, but they will be bittersweet. Creating that culture is an investment in the business. This is true whether you're talking about a restaurant, non-profit organization, or any other company across the board. You must put your focus on bringing in the best people who will surround you, training them properly, making sure they know the expectations, and then allowing them to work in their strength zones.

You must allow people to do great work.

When you do that, leaders will continue to cultivate a culture of excellence that will help raise the bar of performance for everyone on the team, including themselves. When everyone on the team sees the leader put himself on the same level as his team members, in terms of expectations to grow and get better, it empowers the rest of the team and helps fuel the culture of excellence that's being created.

Create, Ideate, and Innovate

When you have that culture of excellence in place, it allows the leader to do three really important things that are critical to enlightened leadership: create, ideate, and innovate. You have to have the time and space to do those things, which can only happen in a culture of excellence. That culture causes you to continually raise the bar of your personal performance and execute at a higher level, going above and beyond your role. Without that culture, you will always be stuck in the muck and the mire of the day-to-day and will never have the time or space to do these three things.

When you are in the sweet spot of a culture of excellence, you're going to be able to create opportunities to help your team members understand and leverage their talents. You're going to be able to help them invest in their talents and direct those strengths towards the initiatives of the organization and allow them to perform at their very best. When a leader is so close to the action that they're able to see their team at that level, it is really inspiring because that means the leader won't become disconnected from the team. They will always be in a position to help the team understand their talents and how to best apply them when they're in this state.

When leaders can look to the future and plan, I think culture also opens an opportunity to ideate. What is the three-year goal?

What are the five- or ten-year goals? You'll be able to ensure that the results you're currently getting are going to fuel that journey. Be in the present but constantly look to the future. **How can I make this better? How can I grow this organization? How can I become better tomorrow than I am today?**

Innovation comes as you are working on ways to invest in that next generation of leadership. *Who's the next person in the organization to grow?* Embrace the ones who are coming up in the organization. This is a hallmark of excellence: to be able to develop talent to be better than you. The person who takes that initiative will always have a role in that organization.

When all those things come together, and you've created that culture of excellence, when you can see things that other people can't and you're able to catch the long-term vision, that's when you're enlightened. That's when you, as an enlightened leader, can take your organization to new heights. Unenlightened leadership can suck the life out of an entire team, but enlightened leadership brings in new life, so you're constantly moving your team forward.

You hear about companies that are innovative, creative, or always looking to the future. When you look at those three qualities together, that is when a company becomes really powerful. They're all necessary. You don't want to be just one or the other. You want to have a good balance of each. Create new ideas, create new opportunities, and create an environment in which the team around you can thrive. That gives you the power to ideate and ask, *what can we bring to life tomorrow that didn't exist today? How can we do that and how can we take it there?* Then there's the idea of innovation—being able to build an environment that learns to do things in new ways for a better result. When an enlightened leader gets to the point when they can seamlessly do these three things, the result is far greater than you would ever expect.

Choose to be that enlightened leader who helps his team members uncover their talents and direct their strengths. Allow them to perform at their very best and create a culture that continues to reinvest in the next generation of leaders, who will never fear surrounding themselves with people who are better than they are.

It Comes Back to the Onion

When I look at the enlightened leader, I circle back to that simple thought from the beginning of the book about cutting an onion. If you look at that onion in the right light, if you position that onion to do exactly the job that you want it to do, you can cut that onion so that you're making the right recipe. Then that onion is going to shine, and it's going to enhance the entire dish that you're creating.

If you take all the things that I've talked about and apply them in the right ways, you will avoid being an unenlightened leader, and you'll avoid allowing an unenlightened leader to stay in your organization. You'll show up the way you're supposed to, and your team will see that. Start by making that transformation in yourself, which will then transform your team, which will then transform your organization.

The way you cut an onion matters. You select the onion, and you carefully peel those layers back while maintaining the root, because the core holds it all together. You make the precise cut that you need for the onion. You're giving a lot of care, attention, and respect to that onion to get it to where you want it to be for whatever it is that you're making.

It's a great analogy for the art of leadership.

You identify the right people, bring them in, care for them, respect them, you help them peel back their layers. *What type of leader are they? How can you help to develop them? How can you help mold them into the best possible leader they can be? How are they going to grow and influence the other leaders they're working with, and how are they going to reproduce themselves? How do they get their leadership to the point where it can be used to influence an entire generation of leaders?*

My journey is no different than yours or anyone else's. We all go through times of learning and times of growth. We go through times of getting it all right and getting it all wrong. **The difference between leadership and great leadership is the ability to figure out when you're doing each** and how to be better at what you do, no matter where you are. I've shared my journey and what I've learned throughout my career with you in hopes of inspiring you to become the best leader you can be. I am so grateful to all the different teams I have been privileged to lead through the years. They have inspired me and made me better!

Challenge yourself as much or more than you challenge your team. Give more than you hold back. Inspire each of your team members to be the best they can be and surround yourself with people who are as talented or more talented than you. Do this and you, your team, and your organization will grow beyond your wildest dreams!

About the Author

Bobby got his start in the restaurant business at McDonald's where he spent seventeen years, starting his career in the kitchen and working his way up to a successful multi-unit leader, before joining Chipotle as an Area Manager. He held various roles in the organization before taking the role of Executive Regional Director in 2008 for the South Region, where he was responsible for 228 restaurants, including opening many new restaurants across 11 states, launching six new markets, and leading the company in many key indicators of performance over the decade he spent with Chipotle.

Since then, Bobby has held a number of senior level executive roles and operates his own restaurant consulting practice through which he teaches leadership development and how to build a great organization by creating strong people cultures. Bobby is also a Gallup Certified Strengths Coach and spends time with leaders helping them learn how to leverage their talents into strengths. He also works with next level leaders helping them to develop their Builder Talents using Gallup's Builder Profile 10 Assessment as they create economic energy in various ventures.

Bobby writes extensively about leadership development on his blog, LinkedIn, and for various restaurant industry trade publications. He also speaks on the topic of leadership development and culture building at various industry conferences.

Bobby and his wife Evan have been married for 25 years and have five amazing children: Jake, Jordan, Joey, Jamisyn, and Jentry. Originally from Kansas City, Bobby and his family now reside in the Austin, Texas area.

For more information please visit:
www.BobbyShawConsulting.com/bookbonuses

Follow Bobby on Twitter @BSC_Consulting.and find him on Facebook at https://www.Facebook.com/bobbyshawconsulting/.

Printed in the USA
CPSIA information can be obtained
at www.ICGtesting.com
JSHW022339140824
68134JS00019B/1571

9 781642 795783